DATE DUE

OC 7 '99			
DE 14 '99			
JE 10 '00			
DE 19 '01			

DEMCO 38-296

THE OTHER MACHIAVELLI

Republican Writings by the Author of "The Prince"

Edited, Introduced, and with an
Essay by

Quentin P. Taylor

University Press of America,® Inc.
Lanham • New York • Oxford

Copyright © 1998 by
America,® Inc.
Way
nd 20706

se Rd.
ord OX2 9JJ

served
Printed in the United States of America
British Library Cataloging in Publication Information Available

Library of Congress Cataloging-in-Publication Data

Machiavelli, Niccolò, 1469-1527.
The other Machiavelli : republican writings by the author of "The
prince" / edited, introduced, and with an essay by Quentin P. Taylor.
p. cm.
Includes bibliographical references.
l. Republicanism—Early works to 1800. 2. Republicanism—Italy—
Florence—History—16th century. 3. Florence (Italy)—Politics and
government—1421-1737. 4. Machiavelli, Niccolò, 1469-1527—
Contributions in republicanism. I. Taylor, Quentin P. II. Title.
JC421.M19   1998   321.8'6 —DC21   97-43868 CIP

ISBN 0-7618-1014-5 (cloth: alk. ppr.)
ISBN 0-7618-1015-3 (pbk: alk. ppr.)

Contents

I beg you to consider how men's affairs develop, and how the power of the world, and especially republics, have developed.

Machiavelli to Franceso Vittori, 1513

Introduction

Niccolò Machiavelli (1469-1527) is best-known to the world as the Italian author of *The Prince*. Written in 1513 and first published in 1532, *Il Principe* soon became the object of burning curiosity and virulent indignation throughout Europe. Both responses had a common source in the novel, shocking, and "demonic" contents of this little book, which along with Machiavelli's other writings was banned by the Catholic Church in 1559. The Church's interdict did not, however, prevent *The Prince* from being widely read; notably among Elizabethans, who with few exceptions (e.g., Francis Bacon) flatly denounced its author as a "counselor of tyrants," an "iconoclast," and a "teacher of evil." To this day "Machiavellism" survives as a universal byword to denote the use of craft, deceit, and ruthlessness in the pursuit of dubious aims. Even those who have never read a word of *The Prince*, "know" that its author's central premise is that "the ends justify the means."

Those more familiar with Machiavelli are aware that *The Prince* is only the most (in)famous of his writings. They also know that he did not restrict his interest to politics, but wrote poetry, plays, histories, and a treatise on warfare. Indeed, had he never penned *Il Principe*, the native Florentine may have been better known to posterity as the author of the popular comic play *Mandragola*. Yet the notoriety of *The Prince* stimulated an interest in Machiavelli's other political writings, of which the *Discourses* is by far the most significant. Indeed, it is on the basis of these two works that Machiavelli's reputation as the "father" of modern political science rests.

The relationship between *The Prince* and the *Discourses* has long been the subject of considerable scholarly debate. It was once tempting to describe the former as a work on principalities, and the latter a treatise on republics. Yet because *The Prince* is often relevant to the state *per se*, and the *Discourses* speaks to principalities as well as republics, this characterization is no longer applied without qualification. What continues to puzzle readers, however, is the odd fact that the same author who gives advice on establishing and preserving one-man rule in *The Prince*, champions the cause of liberty and self-government in the *Discourses*. That Machiavelli possibly interrupted his work on the *Discourses* to write *The Prince* has only complicated the matter. Further obscuring the picture is Machiavelli's fourteen years of tireless service to the Florentine republic, which, among other things, sent him on a series of diplomatic missions to France, Switzerland, Germany, and throughout central Italy. When the republic was dissolved following the return of the exiled Medici in 1512, Machiavelli was dismissed from his post, and shortly thereafter mistakenly implicated in a plot to overthrow the new government, imprisoned, and tortured.

What followed Machiavelli's release from prison has perplexed historians ever since. For as soon as this "republican" patriot gained his freedom, he sought to ingratiate himself with the new regime by writing *The Prince* and dedicating the work to the Medici ruler. Was Machiavelli, as some have suggested, simply a rank opportunist who was willing to betray his republican "principles" in order to gain preferment under a prince? The answer is neither as complex nor sordid as the naked facts suggest. In short, Machiavelli was a political animal of the first order and simply could not bear to remain on the sidelines. Service to Florence, even to a Florence ruled by a prince, was better than wasting his days "in a poor house on a tiny patrimony." The Medici regime was the only game in town, and the erstwhile chancellor desperately wanted a piece of the action.

Opportunism or patriotism? Certainly some of both. But more importantly, Machiavelli's desire to "serve" the Medici was born of a sincere love of country and a healthy confidence in his abilities as a statesman. Moreover, Florence was just then faced with a crisis in international affairs that threatened its very existence as an independent state, princely or republican. Under such conditions, it is not altogether surprising that a man of Machiavelli's experience, insight, and temperament would offer his services to the new order. Finally, the internal political situation in Florence remained fluid for some years after the fall the republic in 1512. Failing to obtain a post, Machiavelli was, nonetheless, among those tapped by the Medici to draft a new constitution for the city-state in 1519. While no reform was forthcoming, the status and stability of the regime remained an open question. In 1527, the year of Machiavelli's death, the Medici were again driven from power, and a republic was once more proclaimed. This would be the last Florentine republic as well as the shortest lived. When the Medici returned in 1530 there was no pretense of maintaining republican forms as had been the case in 1512. Elective posts and popular bodies were abolished, and with them Florentine liberty and self-government.

The foregoing considerations make it easier to understand Machiavelli's "duplicity" in seeking employment under the Medici. It also helps explain the contrast between the republicanism of the *Discourses* and the autocracy of *The Prince*. A better explanation, however, involves a crucial aspect of Machiavelli's thought hinted at above -- *realism*. As one of his biographers has written, what Machiavelli's "extremely dissimilar and sometimes contradictory maxims for action consistently have in common is the goal of the country's well-being (whether under a republican form or not), and their principal instrument is 'the reason of state'." There is no question that Machiavelli strongly preferred *republican* government to any other form, but circumstances were no always conducive to such a regime, nor were all peoples suited to its demands. Today it is political heresy to suggest that a given people may at times be unqualified to govern itself, or that its interests might under certain circumstances be better served by a non-democratic regime. Yet no less a democrat than Jean-Jacques Rousseau affirmed both in his egalitarian manifesto *The Social Contract* (1762). Even today we occasionally hear such thoughts expressed, if only in the hushed tones of forbidden conversation. Is it so shocking, then, to hear them openly stated by someone writing at a time when republics and free cities were the exception and monarchies and principalities the rule?

To trumpet these facts to the world would do much to cleanse the name of Machiavelli of the soot it has been accumulating for more than four centuries. Yet as long as *The Prince* remains the benchmark of opinion, Machiavelli's reputation will continue to suffer under the opprobrium of the ages. Perhaps this is simply the price of *his* fame -- infamy. But would it not surprise a few to learn that this same "child of darkness" was a true "son of liberty"? And would it not strike at conventional wisdom to reveal that this notorious "advisor to princes" was also the father of modern republicanism? Finally, would it not be mildly shocking to discover that the devilish "Old Nick" is in fact the distant ancestor of the American Founding? This book is intended to convey such revelations by bringing to light the *other* Machiavelli. In doing so I hope to counter the popular, and in some cases scholarly, prejudice against one of history's most misunderstood and maligned figures. Conversely, I aim to demonstrate that Machiavelli's positive legacy lies less in his doctrine of *raison d'etat*, than in his philosophy of republican liberty.

To this end one might simply recommend Machiavelli's "book on republics," the *Discourses*. There are, however, a number of problems with this approach. As noted above, Machiavelli's "other book" on politics is not exclusively dedicated to republics, but also addresses monarchies and "princedoms." Moreover, the *Discourses* is a rather lengthy, discursive work, particularly in contrast to the terse, compact *Prince*. The absence of a clear pattern of organization has further militated against its accessibility.

As Edmond Barincou has noted, "instead of the unique, harmonious, well-balanced work that lay within his heart, and well within his powers . . . [Machiavelli] scattered the seed of genius to every wind that blew his way." Finally, there is much in the *Discourses* that no longer speaks to today's reader; much that is of purely historical or antiquarian interest.

Given such obstacles one might despair of ever rendering the "other" Machiavelli accessible to the general reader. Yet with some effort each of these barriers can be overcome. In short, those passages in the *Discourses* (and Machiavelli's other works) which constitute his republican teaching may be isolated, arranged on the basis of subject, and appropriately titled. In addition, relevant historical and biographical references may be identified in a glossary.

Pursuing this editorial strategy achieves the following. First, it reduces the *Discourses* to a fraction of its length by omitting all that does not pertain to the *republican* Machiavelli. (The sections "Man and State" and "Religion and the State" contain discussions of general principles relevant to Machiavelli's republicanism.) In practice, this means deleting many of the specific historical examples he uses to illustrate his general observations. There is, of course, a cost involved here; yet unless the reader is well-versed in Roman history, from which most of Machiavelli's examples are drawn, such references are just as likely to distract as to inform. Moreover, we are less interested in Machiavelli's reflections on the Roman Republic *per se*, than in his republicanism. Rome, however, is not to be ignored, for on the subject of republics, Machiavelli observes, "[t]he example of Rome is preferable to all others." Accordingly, an entire section has been dedicated to his relevant remarks in this area.

Second, our principle of organization brings Machiavelli's republican thought into sharper focus, and allows the reader to easily reference its various features. True, a number of passages could have been assigned to more than one section. In such cases, pride of place has been assigned on the basis of emphasis, and the reader will encounter no real inconvenience due to this mode of arrangement. There are perhaps a few who will object to this "cut and paste" approach to Machiavelli. To these I offer assurances that I have sought to retain the essential meaning of his words by remaining faithful to context. In any event, unabridged editions of the *Discourses*, the *Art of War*, and the *Florentine Histories* are readily available for scholars and specialists. This edition, however, is intended for students, teachers, and citizens, who may rely on its accuracy for purposes of instruction, research, and citation.

Finally, there is the matter of Machiavelli's relation to American republicanism, and in particular the republicanism of the Revolutionary era (1763-1788). As suggested above, it is my contention that the "other" Machiavelli is in many respects the unrecognized "grandfather" of the American republic. This is not to say that Machiavelli's republican writings exercised a direct influence on the Founding Fathers. (In the case of John Adams and a few others, however, they apparently did.) Rather, an actual comparison of these writings with the leading tenets of American republicanism reveals a series of similarities that are at once striking and largely unexpected. While the link between Machiavellian republicanism and the political thought of the Revolutionary period has aroused considerable speculation among scholars, the precise relationship between the two has not been clearly established. In the essay which follows, I set forth the outstanding aspects of this relationship in a systematic manner, drawing on Machiavelli's writings and the works of the Founders. This feature of the book makes it especially relevant to students of American history and government, who may be surprised to find "Old Nick" at the root of their family tree.

It is not my intention to imply that *The Prince* is an anomaly among the Florentine's political writings and should therefore be avoided in favor of the "other" Machiavelli. This would be to assert that there are really "two" Machiavellis, which (although the title of this book begs the conclusion) is not the case here. The peculiar relationship between *The Prince* and its author's republicanism will always remain something of a puzzle. However, I have found it useful to view *The Prince* as a special instance of Machiavelli's political *science*, and the *Discourses* as the core of this science, as well as the heart of the Florentine's political *philosophy*. If this characterization is valid, Professor Bull's assertion that "Machiavelli was fundamentally interested in the state, rather than in the form of its government" requires qualification, for it suggests an *indifference* to forms that did not really exist. Machiavelli was, of course, a shrewd observer of men and possessed a notable capacity for dispassionate analysis. Yet he also expressed an unmistakable commitment to the principle of ordered liberty under a just and stable republic. Unfortunately, this aspect of the Florentine's life and thought has been (outside of specialists) almost totally eclipsed by the influence of *The Prince*. To highlight the "other" Machiavelli, the Machiavelli who is the kindred of all who place a premium on liberty and self-government, would therefore appear not only justified but fitting.

Note on the Text

Selections from the *Discourses* (*D*), translated by Christian E. Detmold, adopted from the Modern Library edition of *The Prince and the Discourses* (New York, 1950). Machiavelli's rather lengthy chapter titles have been omitted. Roman and Arabic numerals following selections indicate book and chapter number in the original. Selections from *The Art of War* (*AW*) translated by Ellis Farnsworth, revised by Neal Wood (New York, 1965). Arabic numerals indicate chapter number. Remaining selections adopted from *Machiavelli: The Chief Works and Others*, translated by Allan Gilbert, 3 vols. (Durham, N. C., 1965), and reprinted here with the kind permission of Duke University Press. These are "A Discourse on Remodeling the Government of Florence" (*GF*); "A Provision for Infantry" (*PI*); "Words to be Spoken on the Law for Appropriating Money" (*AM*); and *The History of Florence* (*HF*). Selections from *HF* are followed by book and chapter numbers. Spelling and punctuation have been standardized, but no substantive changes have been made in the translations.

Machiavelli and the American Republic

I. Introduction

Since the publication of J. G. A. Pocock's *The Machiavellian Moment* (1975), Niccolò Machiavelli has assumed a notable presence in the ongoing debate over the "ideological" character of the American Founding. The debate itself is often traced to Charles Beard's provocative and influential *An Economic Interpretation of the Constitution of the United States* (1913). More recently, scholars have shifted their attention from a preoccupation with the ulterior motives of the Framers (the focus of Beard's study) in order to investigate the broader intellectual currents that shaped the political and constitutional thought of the Revolutionary era. Among the first fruits of this reorientation were seminal works by historians Bernard Bailyn (1967) and Gordon Wood (1969).[1] These now classic studies stimulated an impressive renewal of interest in the political ideas of the American Founding; a renewal further invigorated by Pocock's "magisterial" study. Indeed, the conceptual and methodological innovations introduced by these scholars, as well as their substantive findings, continue to frame much of the debate on the sources, meaning, and evolution of early American political thought.

The main point of contention in this dialogue has been the importance scholars have attached to various traditions in shaping the political "language" of the Revolutionary generation. By all accounts these traditions are diverse, intersect and overlap, and in some cases date back to classical antiquity. Sorting out the different strands of thought and recasting them in their American context has, accordingly, presented even the most gifted scholars with a formidable challenge. Among Professor Wood's salient contributions was to show that one of these strands -- "classical republicanism" -- was not only distinct from the "liberal" tradition represented by John Locke (1632-1704), but was basically opposed to its "individualistic" assumptions and values. Building on this distinction, Wood concluded that classical republicanism was not only widespread in the political thinking of the time, but was on the whole more pervasive than Lockean liberalism.[2]

While Wood tacitly identified Machiavelli as a distant source of American republicanism, it was Professor Pocock who traced the "neo-classical" tradition in Anglo-American thought to its roots in the civic humanism of Renaissance Florence.[3] By way of establishing this genealogical connection, Pocock explored the nature and role of republican "ideology" in seventeenth and eighteenth-century England,[4] and underscored the profound, and largely unrecognized, influence of "Machiavellian" thought (if not Machiavelli himself) in early American politics.[5]

Given the long-standing prevalence of the Lockean "paradigm" among students of the Founding era, it is not surprising that the ambitious scope and novel findings of Wood and Pocock's studies generated considerable controversy. Yet for all the ink spilled on "classical republicanism" and the "Machiavellian moment," the specific relation between *Machiavelli's* republicanism and the republicanism of the American Founding has remained largely undefined. In part this is due to the fact that most of the pioneering work in this area has been done by intellectual historians as opposed to political theorists. As such, the former have been primarily interested in identifying various patterns of political thought and illustrating how the character and transformation of these "responses" reflected salient tensions in the broader social and economic order. Given their sensitivity to "social context" and "conceptual paradigms," the historians have generally been critical of the ostensibly ahistorical and procrustean approach employed by political theorists. For their part, the theorists (particularly those of the "perennial issues" persuasion) have accused the historians of reductionism and superficiality in their treatment of political ideas.[6]

Like most debates which involve scholars across disciplines, this one has produced its share of misunderstandings. Many on both sides have simply failed to recognize the inherent differences in the respective tasks of the intellectual historian and the political theorist. The historian is typically involved in extrapolating a meaning or significance *beyond* the text, while the theorist is generally interested in the nature and value of the ideas *therein*. Clearly, each approach constitutes a legitimate enterprise, with its own particular strengths and limitations. Much undue controversy could be averted if this simple distinction were acknowledged and respected.

With these considerations in mind, we may turn to the subject of this essay: the *republican* Machiavelli's relation to the American Founding. Yet before proceeding a few words of clarification are in order. First, what follows is primarily informed by the methods and concerns of the political theorist. Accordingly, it is not my intention to establish the *presence* of "Machiavellian" thought in early American politics, or to speculate as to its *influence* on the Founding generation. Rather, I aim to *compare* Machiavelli's republican teaching with the republicanism of the Revolutionary era in order to establish more precisely the *relationship* between the two.

This task is complicated by the fact that political thought in early America, while marked by a broad consensus on fundamentals, exhibited a degree of diversity on many particulars. In short, the Founding period was characterized by more than one strain of republicanism. This raises the question of what sources should be relied upon for comparing the republican Machiavelli with the "republicanism" of the Founding: those which reflect the predominance of Lockean liberalism? or Calvinist covenant theory? or "classical" republicanism? or Scottish philosophy? or English common law? Or should one simply enlist the principles and provisions contained in the early state constitutions? or in the U. S. Constitution? or the ideas of its original defenders and detractors, the Federalists and Antifederalists? Alternatively, one might link the components of Machiavelli's republican theory to corresponding expressions in the American context; or posit an "ideal-type" of American republicanism and compare its generic features with the republican aspects of Machiavelli's thought.

Our choice in this matter will largely turn on the following: a consideration of Machiavelli's republican doctrines; recognition that pride of place should be given to that species of republicanism that ultimately triumphed in America (viz., the republicanism of the state and federal constitutions, and *The Federalist Papers*); and convenience of presentation. Informed by these guidelines I propose to (1) list the essential tenets of American republicanism (e.g., popular sovereignty, constitutionalism, rule of law) and determine if there is a corresponding doctrine for each in Machiavelli; (2) explore some additional areas of convergence (e.g., faction, civic virtue) between the Florentine's thought and that of the Founders; and (3) identify those features of Machiavelli's republican thought (e.g., dictatorship, the sole legislator) which appear to find no corresponding expression in *any* variety of American republicanism. In this manner, I hope to establish the kinship of Machiavelli's republicanism with that of the Revolutionary era. We will then be in a position to judge the degree to which the Florentine *anticipated* the political teaching(s) of the American Founders.

II. Machiavelli and the Tenets of Republicanism

The authoritative sources for the leading tenets of American republicanism are the Declaration of Independence and the state and federal constitutions. The records of the Philadelphia Convention and the ratification debates, as well as *The Federalist Papers*, represent the most authoritative commentaries on these tenets. In these "sacred" documents it is possible to identify at least a dozen distinct (yet closely related) republican principles. Following a brief statement of each, we will turn to Machiavelli in search of a corresponding endorsement.

1. **Popular Sovereignty**   The notion that ultimate political authority resides with "the people" (or a majority thereof) is the master concept of republicanism, American or otherwise. The reference in the Declaration of Independence to the necessity for "one people" to terminate its political relationship with another is an implicit expression of this idea. The corollary of popular sovereignty, that governments derive "their just powers from the consent of the governed," also appears in the Declaration, as well as in the preambles of many of the first state constitutions.[7] Ultimately these twin pillars of republicanism were enshrined in the U. S. Constitution in three simple but majestic words: "We the People."

One will not find an equally unambiguous statement of popular sovereignty (or consent) in Machiavelli. As a political thinker who attempted to ground his theorizing in abiding realities, the concept would likely have struck him as a questionable abstraction. Indeed, while the doctrine of popular sovereignty was embraced by some of his Italian predecessors and Protestant contemporaries, it would not receive full theoretical elaboration until the seventeenth century. Instead of "sovereignty," Machiavelli speaks of "power" (*potestà*) and "authority" (*autorità*), which he often equates with political right. That he considers "the people" a source of authority is, however, repeatedly implied in the *Discourses*. For example, the Florentine notes that under the Roman Republic (which he takes as his model), "[t]he constitution of the state reposed upon the authority of the people (*L'ordine dello Stato era l'autorità del Popolo*), the Senate, the Tribunes, and the Consuls." (*D*, I:18). Elsewhere, Machiavelli tacitly associates the "supreme and absolute authority in a free state" (*volere pigliare autorità in una republica*) with "the people." (*D*, III:8)[8]

Insofar as Machiavelli was a legal positivist, this last passage should not be read as an endorsement of popular sovereignty *in abstracto*.[9] In practice, however, the Florentine's commitment to republicanism entails an acceptance of the principle that sovereign *autorità* resides with the people as a whole. This can be seen in his (1) endorsement of popular elections based on "the free suffrages of the people" (*D*, I:35), (2) repeated references to the "common benefit" and "general good" (*D*, II:2), (3) emphasis on the need for popular participation in republics (*GF*; *D*, I:18), and (4) defense of the "the people" *vis-à-vis* the nobility and the prince. (*D*, I:47, I:58, III:34) In conjunction, these features of Machiavelli's republicanism lead to the conclusion that the citizens of a republic are indeed sovereign; for in a republic "the people have power" (*il popolo abbia autorità*). (*D*, I:53)

2. *Natural Rights* In their dispute with Great Britain during the 1760s and 1770s, the American colonists incessantly invoked the "rights of Englishmen" in their declamations against the policies of king and parliament. Such "rights" were traditionally seen as emanating from English common law and the "Ancient Constitution," and received their sanction from statute or custom. The "rights of Englishmen," then, were largely *prescriptive* in nature and *limited* in their application. In order to encourage emigration, such traditional rights as jury trial were extended to the first English colonists in America. And while the principle of prescriptive right remained vital throughout the eighteenth century, it was progressively supplemented, and ultimately supplanted, by the doctrine of natural rights, which began to gain currency in the mid-seventeenth century. In contrast to prescriptive or customary rights (i.e., man-made conventions hallowed by usage), "natural" rights were understood to be inherent in man. Given their ultimate source in "natural law" (created by God and grasped by reason), natural rights were considered both "unalienable" and "universal." In John Locke's classic formulation, the rights of "life, liberty, and estate" are among mankind's original and native possessions. The chief end of government is (or should be) the protection of these "natural" rights.[10]

In British North America these two traditions of rights, prescriptive and natural, had begun to merge by the mid-1700s. Accordingly, when the colonists denounced parliament for transgressions against their "ancient rights," this often implied a violation of their "natural" rights as well. Yet as Americans drew closer to independence, appeals to the "Ancient Constitution" became less compelling, and greater recourse was had to the more radical "natural" rights doctrine. It was the latter that triumphed when the formal decision to sever ties with the mother country was taken in the summer of 1776. From that moment forward, the notion that all men are "endowed with certain unalienable rights," including "life, liberty, and the pursuit of happiness," has stood as the chief article of the American creed.

Turning to Machiavelli we find no doctrine of "natural" rights among the articles of his republican faith. Indeed, it is difficult to discover any doctrine of "rights" whatsoever in his writings.[11] By implication, however, "rights" for Machiavelli have their origin in law, which supports the view that the Florentine was a legal positivist.[12] Unlike Thomas Hobbes (1588-1679) and Locke, the fathers of natural rights theory, Machiavelli depicts the pre-political "state of nature" in historical terms. Whatever "justice" actually emerged from this condition was not the product of a "social compact," whereby rights-bearing individuals "consent" to forego their "natural" liberty in exchange for the security of "civil society."[13] Rather, "the origin of justice," according to Machiavelli, was coeval with the creation of laws and with "punishments for those who contravened them."

(*D*, I:2) The basis of government, then, is purely conventional; rooted in the human desire for survival and the determination to "prevent . . . evils." Here the Florentine is not so far from Hobbes and Locke after all, for each maintains that men enter into civil society to escape the "inconveniences" of the pre-political state: indeed, it is wholly "natural" for them to do so. Yet Machiavelli's failure to recognize the existence of universal, unalienable, "natural" rights *à la* Locke and Jefferson admittedly outweighs this similarity. For once the doctrine of "natural" rights -- whether fictitious or not -- is abandoned (or merely ignored), the sanctity and security of the individual is thereby placed in jeopardy. Yet as with popular sovereignty, Machiavelli's practical commitments to liberty, security, and limited government bring him into a closer relationship with American republicanism than his silence on the issue of "rights" might otherwise suggest.

3. ***The Rule of Law***   The rule of law is by no means exclusive to republican government; strictly speaking it is compatible with almost any type of regime. In its common usage, however, the rule of law denotes a prohibition on the arbitrary exercise of power, particularly on the part of public officials. It was just such an alleged abuse of authority by Parliament and George III that led the American colonists to declare their independence from Great Britain. Indeed, the series of "injuries and usurpations" catalogued in the Declaration of Independence reads like a litany on arbitrary rule. Consequently, in framing their constitutions Americans were particularly concerned with devising the means of preventing similar abuses in their own systems of government. In so doing, they could boast with John Adams that, "ours is a government of laws, not men." Subsequently, the rule of law has been a hallmark of American republicanism.

Upon no principle of government is Machiavelli more insistent than the rule of law. Even his commitment to republican liberty stands in an inferior position, for he does not believe that all peoples, at all times are capable of governing themselves.[14] In such cases, some form of monarchy is required for the welfare of the community. Yet in both instances, adherence to law is for Machiavelli the desideratum of good government and a bar to arbitrary rule, whether by mob or despot. When circumstances did not favor a republican system, a monarchy in which the prince is constrained by law is the appropriate model. (*D*, I:18) Under such a regime (i.e., limited monarchy), the security of the individual, as well as a reasonable measure of personal liberty, can be harmonized with the "rule" of a single individual. (*D*, I:16, I:58; *Prince*, XIX)[15]

In the *Discourses*, Machiavelli emphasizes the importance of the rule of law with respect to republics, and rightly regards this principle as the touchstone of liberty. This is evident in his contention that "it [is] inconsistent with a proper regard for liberty to violate the law . . . For I think that there can be no worse example in a republic than to make a law and not observe it." (*D*, I:45) Elsewhere he predicts that if the factions in a republic "do not agree to secure liberty by law" (*a fare una legge in favore della libertà*), and one party turns to a strongman to crush its opponents, "a tyranny is the natural result." (*D*, I:40) Even deviations from the law "for good objects" must be prevented, for "the precedent is pernicious" and can only lead to usurpations "under that pretext." (*D*, I:34) Moreover, Machiavelli anticipates the First Amendment in his contention that citizens should be authorized by law to petition their government for redress of grievances. (*D*, I:49) More generally, "every citizen [should] have the right to accuse another citizen without fear or suspicion." (*D*, I:8)[16] Finally, the law should apply to all equally, and those duly convicted of violating it should be "punished without regard to person." (*D*, I:7) Clearly, on the subject of the rule of law, Machiavelli may be placed squarely in the company of the Founders.

4. **Equality** When Thomas Jefferson declared that "all men are created equal," he gave expression to one of history's most revolutionary ideas. He was not, of course, asserting the physical, moral, or intellectual equivalency of men. Indeed, Jefferson saw nothing inconsistent in championing the "natural" and "equal" rights of man, while simultaneously proclaiming the existence and desirability of a "natural aristocracy" of "virtue" and "talent." For Jefferson and most Americans, equality meant primarily an equality of rights or equality under the law. As historian Joel Barlow wrote in 1792, the driving force behind the Revolution, and the key to sustaining freedom in America was the belief "*that all men are equal in their rights.*"[17] Admittedly, this principle was limited in its application at the time of the Founding, but for those to whom it did apply, such equality was synonymous with liberty itself.

Insofar as the American concept of equality was rooted in natural law theory, one should not expect to find this doctrine among Machiavelli's republican *de fides*. As in the case of popular sovereignty and natural rights, a clear expression of "natural" equality would not appear (at least in England) until the seventeenth century. Accordingly, Machiavelli approaches equality not as an inherent, "natural" quality men possess *qua* men, but rather as a function of custom (or psychology) and historical circumstance. As for the former, he was at one with Barlow, who claimed that equality in America was first and foremost a "habit of thinking." Where this "habit" is missing, the Florentine suggests, republican government will seldom if ever thrive. Conversely, "in all cities where the citizens are accustomed to equality (*egualità*), a princedom cannot be set up except with utmost difficulty." (*GF*). Equality thus understood is among the vital prerequisites of republicanism. "Let republics, then, be established where equality exists." (*D*, I:55)

Machiavelli's strong preference for republican government implies an attachment to the principle of equality. His commitment to this principle is revealed more directly as well. We have noted Machiavelli's reverence for the rule of law and its unbiased application to all citizens. Elsewhere he states that the establishment of a republican regime requires the elimination of special privileges for the few. (*D*, I:55; *GF*) Furthermore, Machiavelli embraces the principle of meritocracy; i.e., that honors, including public office, "should be open to every citizen." (*D*, III:28) Like Jefferson, the Florentine's notion of equality "is not economic or social, but legal and political, meaning equality before the law and equal access to public office . . ."[18] Machiavelli does, however, suggest that it may be necessary to reserve "the highest offices in the republic" for the wealthy (*GF*). Yet nearly all of the early state constitutions mandated property qualifications for elected officials, which in some cases restricted office-holding to a narrow oligarchy. This "exception" aside, there is little doubt that Machiavelli viewed equality as the corollary of freedom, for like the Founders, he maintained that only in a republic could "liberty and equality prevail." (*D*, I:55)

5. *Limited Government* Since a group of discomfited barons compelled King John to sign the Magna Carta in 1215, English-speaking peoples have sought to limit the power and scope of their governments. The preferred method has been the charter or constitution, a written statement of the "legitimate" powers of government as well as the privileges and immunities enjoyed by "subjects" or citizens. The aim of such documents was not merely to formalize what had hitherto been sanctioned by custom, but more importantly to place limits on the exercise of public authority. To enumerate the prerogatives of sovereignty was, by implication, to limit them, and many early charters contained explicit prohibitions which even the sovereign was obliged to respect.

The doctrine of limited government is premised on a belief in the sanctity of individual rights, and speaks to the existence of a sphere that should largely be free of governmental intrusion. Even the authoritarian Hobbes recognized a number of areas where individuals should be left to their own discretion.[19] In declaring that governments are created to secure "life, liberty, and the pursuit of happiness," Jefferson and his countrymen pushed this notion to its logical conclusion. The list of charges brought against George III, whose actions ostensibly aimed at "the establishment of an absolute tyranny," underscored a fervent belief that all power must be limited. This belief was given formal expression in America's constitutions and bills of rights.

As an advocate of liberty, equality, and the rule of law, Machiavelli implicitly embraced the principle of limited government. This commitment is also apparent in his constitutionalism, which will be discussed below. On occasion, however, the Florentine explicitly endorses limited government, as in the following passage, where he argues that elected officials should be restricted in their powers and term of office.

> . . . when we said that an authority conferred by the free suffrages of the people never harmed a republic, we presupposed that the people, in giving that power would limit it (*non si conduca mai a darla*), as well as the time during which it was to be exercised. (*D*, I:35)

Elsewhere Machiavelli distinguishes between private, foreign, and public "force," and notes that in a healthy republic the last operates "in accordance with the established laws, which have their prescribed limits that cannot be transcended" (*che hanno i termini loro particulari, né transcendono*). (*D*, I:7) Even monarchs are obliged, under normal circumstances, to refrain from arbitrary measures, especially confiscations, excessive taxation, and the violation of women. (*Prince*, XVI, XIX) In combination with related aspects of the Florentine's republicanism, these provisions clearly indicate that, like the Founders, Machiavelli firmly subscribed to the doctrine of limited government.

6. *Constitutionalism* It is well-known that the demand for limited government in America took the form of written documents called "constitutions." Yet prior to the Revolutionary era, the word "constitution" was used rather loosely to signify either a "complex of government" or a state's "fundamental laws," as opposed to a specific document. For instance, when the colonists invoked the "Ancient Constitution" in defense of their rights as British subjects, they were not referring to a single "written" constitution, but to the statutory and customary protections acquired over the course of time. The decade long assault on these rights by parliament and king convinced many Americans that the traditional "rights of Englishmen" required especial protections. When the time for action came, most of the Revolutionary legislatures drafted constitutions which established the frames of government and fundamental law for their respective states. (The Articles of Confederation was drafted by a committee of the Continental Congress in 1777 and formally adopted by the states in 1781.) Distinct from and superior to the simple statutes passed by legislative bodies, the

American constitutions embodied the principle of "organic" or "higher" law. As such, the specific contents of these constitutions could neither be repealed nor amended by ordinary legislation, executive order, or judicial ruling. On the basis of these unique features, the American Founders are often credited with having drafted and adopted the first written constitutions.

Like the Founders, Machiavelli distinguishes between a republic's "constitution" (*ordini*) and its "laws" (*legge*), yet he does not appear to have adopted their precise definition of the relation between the two.[20] For the Florentine, the *ordini* of a "state" (*stato*) encompasses its political institutions, public offices (including length of term, duties, mode of selection), and rules of lawmaking. As such the *ordini* (or *constituzione*) embodies the institutional and procedural facets of a government. The substantive side of politics takes the form of laws, ordinances, judicial rulings, and executive enactments. Given this distinction one should not expect to find the doctrine of "higher" or constitutional law in Machiavelli. What one does find, however, are the seeds of such a doctrine. For in discussing the Roman constitution, Machiavelli asserts that a leading cause of the Republic's fall was the fact that its laws were "not in harmony with the constitution." (*D*, I:18) However, instead of adopting a "higher law" doctrine (and its corollary of judicial review) to prevent such an imbalance, he suggests that the *ordini* itself "should be amended (*innovare*), either all at once, or by degrees as each defect becomes known." (*D*, I:18)

From his remarks in this area it appears that Machiavelli was groping toward a form of constitutionalism not altogether unlike the American brand. For example, he indicates that institutional and procedural forms alone are insufficient to check the passage of bad laws. For once a people has become "corrupt" (to use Machiavelli's favorite example), there is nothing to restrain it or its leaders from proposing and adopting measures inimical to liberty and good government. The solution to his dilemma, apparent to those who framed America's first constitutions, was to incorporate certain substantive safeguards into an organic document not subject to modification by the ordinary channels of legislation. Machiavelli does not explicitly adopt this solution, but he does suggest that a state's basic laws should be comprehensive, thus implying that a constitution should be more than merely a formal device for governing. "[N]o republic will ever be perfect," he asserts, "if she has not by law provided for everything, having a remedy for every emergency, and fixed rules for applying it" (*e dato il modo a governarlo*). (*D*, I:34)

In the end, however, the Florentine advocates modifications in the "constitution" itself; that is, in institutions and procedures, as opposed to giving greater weight to a fundamental law. (*D*, III:9, I:18) To achieve the former and maintain the republican form is, however, probably "impossible;" and for this reason Machiavelli despairs of ever reforming a corrupt republic via republican means. (*D*, I:18) Having failed to discover a remedy for "corruption" in a substantive "higher" law, he is brought to lament "how difficult it is in the constitution (*ordinare*) of a republic to provide necessary laws for the maintenance of liberty." (*D*, I:49)

7. *Judicial Review* As noted above, the American Founders recognized the difference between organic law as embodied in their constitutions and the statutory enactments of their legislatures. This distinction, with its roots in the colonial charters, first found clear expression in the early state constitutions. Implicit in these documents, which secured both civil liberties and political rights, was the doctrine of *judicial review*; the power of the courts to void any act or law that conflicted with or infringed upon the "higher" law embodied in the constitution. Prior to the adoption of the Federal Constitution in 1788, the power of judicial review gained formal recognition in a number of states, although not without opposition from defenders of legislative supremacy. Judicial review was also implicitly incorporated into the U. S. Constitution, and explicitly affirmed by the authors of *The Federalist*. In the landmark case of *Marbury v. Madison* (1803), the doctrine entered into constitutional orthodoxy when the Supreme Court struck down an act of Congress for the first time. More recently, actions taken by the executive branch have been subjected to judicial scrutiny, and occasionally held unconstitutional by the federal courts.

As noted above, Machiavelli did not have a clear understanding of a constitution as a fundamental law which ordinary statutes could neither violate nor alter. Accordingly, the principle of judicial review is absent from his writings. But just as he tacitly recognizes the need for constitutional guarantees and safeguards, he suggests that such provisions must be defended against attack. In the *Discourses*, Machiavelli asserts that "in a well-ordered republic it should never be necessary to resort to extra-constitutional measures" (*modi straordinari si avesse a governare*). (*D*, I:34) This statement is backed by a specific provision in his plan for remodeling the Florentine government, which was drafted at the request of Pope Leo X in 1519. Here Machiavelli argues that upon the death of the pope (who under the plan was to have an absolute negative on all "official" enactments), it will be necessary to establish a body (or bodies) vested with a similar power. Hence if some department of the government "does things opposed to the common good through wickedness, somebody may be at hand to take from them that power and appeal their decision to another body." (*GF*) And while Machiavelli does not specify the precise (judicial) nature of this "body," or invoke the concept of "higher" law, his recommendation for appealing to a third party suggests that he sensed the necessity of something *like* judicial review in order to check encroaching legislators and overzealous executives. His admiration for the *parlements*, the supreme courts of law in France whose authority limited royal power, further supports the inference.[21]

8. *Separation of Powers* The firm conviction that a concentration of power in the hands of a single individual (or body of men) was "precisely the definition of despotic government,"[22] led Americans to deliberately divide power into different branches or departments. The first state constitutions were notably explicit in this regard. The Virginia Constitution, for example, stipulated that "[t]he legislative, executive, and judiciary department, shall be separate and distinct, so that neither exercise the powers properly belonging to the other." Such a division, however, did not imply a *total* separation, which would destroy the necessary unity of government. (More accurately, the American constitutions reflected the principle of *blended* powers.) Nor did the first state constitutions contemplate an equal division of powers among the three departments, but typically embodied the prevailing doctrine of "legislative supremacy." In some states this led to an undue preponderance of legislative authority, which gave rise to class-based politics and the "tyranny of the majority." By the time the U. S. Constitution was ratified, a number of states had corrected this imbalance by shifting authority to the executive branch and establishing the practice of judicial review.

The Philadelphia Constitution also incorporated the principle of separation of powers. Again this meant neither a strict separation in all powers, nor a crude equality of power among the three branches. While it was essential for each department to fulfill its proper constitutional role, the Framers assumed that the legislative department would in many respects function as the cardinal branch of government.

For his part, Machiavelli recognized the distinction between the legislative, executive, and judicial functions of government, but does not appear to have understood the separation of powers in the manner of the Founders. Yet insofar as the separation of powers was embodied by his two favorite republics, Rome and Sparta, it cannot be said that Machiavelli was blind to its meaning or value. On the other hand, his plan for revising the government of Florence fails to provide a conscious division of powers on the American model. Indeed, Machiavelli's proposed "constitution" creates a hodgepodge of offices and bodies with overlapping functions and blurred jurisdictions.[23] He does advocate streamlining the existing Florentine government, including the elimination of its "jumble of councils." Not only are such bodies unnecessary, he argues, they are susceptible to the rage of "factions" (*sette*). (*GF*) Such concerns, however, do not add up to a doctrine of separation of powers.

In failing to clearly distinguish and divide the functions of government, Machiavelli was hardly alone, for it was not until the late seventeenth century that the doctrine of separation of powers was clearly expressed by John Locke. It can not, then, be said that the Florentine anticipated the American Founders in this regard. Nevertheless, this "omission" must be balanced against Machiavelli's related doctrine of checks and balances.

9. *Checks and Balances* In *Notes on the State of Virginia*, Thomas Jefferson observed that "the powers of government should be so divided and balanced among several bodies of magistracy, as that none could transcend their legal limits, without being effectively checked and restrained by the others."[24] Even before Jefferson penned these words in 1781, many Americans recognized the necessity of fortifying their new governments with a system of "checks and balances," although they did not typically use this expression. Given the colonists' experience with high-handed royal governors, the first state constitutions predictably focused on restraining executive power. This was achieved by providing for (1) a governor elected by the legislature, (2) limitations on eligibility for and term of office, (3) a simple majority to override a veto, and (4) restrictions on the power of appointment. These and other measures hedged executive authority to the point of undermining the separation of powers. Moreover, outside of the internal "check" of bicameralism (except in Georgia and Pennsylvania which had unicameral legislatures), there was little in the early state constitutions capable of withstanding the "impetuous vortex" of legislative authority.

A decade of political turbulence convinced many Americans that an unchecked legislature could be just as inimical to liberty and good government as an unrestrained executive. As noted above, a number of states, before and after the Federal Convention, made important revisions in their constitutions which strengthened the powers of the executive *vis-à-vis* the legislative branch. Moreover, between 1787 and 1803 state courts nullified over twenty legislative acts, thus institutionalizing the additional check of judicial review.

In the U. S. Constitution the "science" of checks and balances reached an unprecedented level of refinement. In a series of intricate measures, the Framers provided the means for each branch to limit the power of the others, as well as protect itself from unwarranted encroachments into its proper sphere of authority. The internal workings of the national government are well-known to those acquainted with the Constitution and need not be enumerated here. Suffice it to say that, while the system of checks and balances has not always succeeded in checking undue incursions, it has typically succeeded in restoring the desired balance.

Machiavelli's clearest statement of the doctrine of checks and balances appears in the context of his remarks on the mixed regime, a government comprised of monarchical, aristocratic, and democratic elements. The Greek historian Polybius (c. 201-120 B.C.), whom Machiavelli draws heavily upon in this area, believed that the greatness of Rome lay chiefly in its political institutions, and particularly in the blending of the three "pure" forms of government.[25] In this view, the monarchical element was supplied by the consuls and other high magistrates, the aristocratic principle by the senate, and the democratic aspect by the tribunes (who defended the rights of the plebeians) and popular assemblies. When these three elements interacted with and "balanced" one another, the constitution may be described as a "mixed" or "composite" one.

While there is some discrepancy between this typology and Roman reality, it is clear that Machiavelli warmly embraced the mixed constitution as the best means of channeling diverse societal interests and restraining the principal social classes. On this basis, he concludes that "when there is combined under the same constitution a prince, a nobility, and the power of the people, then these three powers will watch and keep each other reciprocally in check" (*giudicandolo piú fermo e piú stabile, perché l'uno guarda l'altro*). (*D*, I:2)

There is admittedly a notable difference between a system which seeks to limit power via a balance of social forces and one that does so on the basis of a series of specific constitutional provisions. Yet it is evident that Machiavelli envisaged a republican regime that would effectively check the abuse of power by employing elements of both.[26] Since he takes "the constitution of Rome as a model," it is likely that he endorsed those aspects (e.g., tribunate, senate) which provided formal or internal means of restraining the power of the other "branches" of government. Moreover, Machiavelli's constitution for Florence contains such provisions as executive veto, legislative delay, and a procedure resembling judicial review. Finally, there are a number of passages where Machiavelli clearly recognizes the necessity for institutional checks on the exercise of authority. For example, he recommends that when citizens establish a magistracy, "they should do it in such a way that the magistrates should have some hesitation before they abuse their powers." (*D*, I:40) More generally, however, it is "not good that officeholders should not have somebody to observe them and make them abstain from actions that are not good." (*GF*)

Such observations indicate that Machiavelli plainly recognized the vital importance of constitutional provisions designed to keep one element of the government (or populace) from overwhelming the others, and thus destroying the "balance" of social and political forces. This reading finds support in Machiavelli's plan for creating a balanced regime in Florence. Here he declares: "There is no other way for escaping these ills [of unchecked faction] than to give to the city institutions that can by themselves stand firm." (*GF*) And while the means he devised appear less than ideally suited to perform this function, Machiavelli clearly saw the necessity of placing checks on the various agencies of government in order to forestall abuses and achieve a "balanced" polity.

10. ***Mixed Government*** Since the adoption of the U. S. Constitution there has been some confusion as to whether or not the Framers established a "mixed" government. One can find occasional references to the concept in the records of the Federal Convention. For example, some delegates viewed the proposed lower house as "the grand depository of the democratic principle," the upper house as "having a dangerous tendency to aristocracy," and the executive as containing the "foetus of monarchy."[27] Such language indicates not merely a familiarity with the categories of classical political analysis, but a belief that the Constitution established a kind of *mixed* regime. More specifically, their strictures leveled at an ostensible excess of the monarchical or aristocratic "principle," spoke to a common fear that any one of these elements would subvert and overpower the others. It is plausible that those who voiced this concern understood the task of constitution-making in terms of balancing the so-called democratic, aristocratic, and monarchical elements of government, and thus creating the "equilibrium" of the mixed regime.

On the other hand, the Framers did not view the House of Representatives, the Senate, or the Presidency in terms of corresponding social classes, which had no recognition in American law. Rather, their use of "monarchical," "aristocratic," and "democratic" in characterizing the Constitution spoke to the principles and composition of the actual government. Moreover, the Framers faced the difficult task of incorporating the interests of the state governments into the make-up of the national government. This was a largely matter of blending *national* and *federal* principles, rather than balancing the "pure" forms of government. This said, it may still be argued that the authors of the American constitutions erected frames of government that partook of monarchical, aristocratic, and democratic *principles*, and to this degree established "mixed" polities.

We have seen that Machiavelli adopted the classical Polybian doctrine of the mixed regime, a doctrine whose roots may be traced to Plato and

Aristotle.[28] It was the Florentine's belief that "[t]hose who organize a republic ought to provide for the three different sorts of men who exist in all cities, namely, the most important, those in the middle, and the lowest." (*GF*) Yet given Machiavelli's emphasis on *equality* and *merit*, it is difficult to reconcile a class-based scheme of representation with the general tendency of his republicanism. The reason for this discrepancy, however, may in part be ascribed to the context in which this recommendation was made. As Machiavelli observes, while a formal equality prevails in Florence, "some of her citizens have ambitious spirits (*animo elevato*) and think they deserve to outrank the others; these must be satisfied in organizing the republic." (*GF*) In such cases, it is necessary to reserve "the highest offices in the republic" for "men of this sort" in the interest of reconciling the nobles (*grandi*) to a republican regime.

Just how to accomplish this end without creating legal classifications among the citizenry (thereby undermining the strict republican character of the regime) is a problem Machiavelli fails to adequately address. Yet even as he hints at this "elitist" solution, he remains hostile to anything approaching an oligarchic government dominated by the few. For "[w]ithout satisfying the generality of the citizens (*all' universale*), to set up a stable government is always impossible." (*GF*) In a true republic, such satisfaction will require more than the guarantee of certain "protections" short of tangible political rights. Rather, "satisfying" the *popolo* demands recognition in the form of explicit representation and an opportunity to participate in the political life of the commonwealth. In conjunction with the representatives of the remaining social classes, a mixed regime will function so as to sustain its *ordini* in a dynamic, yet harmonious balance.[29] For the institutions of such a republic "will always stand firm when everybody has a hand in them, and when everybody knows what he needs to do and in whom he can trust, and no class of citizens, either through fear for itself or through ambition, will need to desire revolution" (*innovazione*). (*GF*)

11. **Representation** The principle of representation is nearly synonymous with republicanism itself, and as James Madison observed, distinguishes a *republic* from a (direct or pure) *democracy*. (*Federalist* No. 10) Instead of permitting a majority of citizens to determine public matters by direct vote, or selecting officials by lot (the practice in Rome and Athens), the American constitutions called upon the voters to select a small number of "delegates" or "representatives" who would govern on their behalf. Suspicious of executive power (and in some cases of the people themselves), the authors of the first constitutions (except in New York and Massachusetts) vested the power of choosing the governor not with the electorate, but with

the legislature. Nor did they provide for popular election of state judges. Yet since the legislature was widely seen as the embodiment of the "will of the people," these prohibitions were not considered inconsistent with the principle of popular sovereignty. Only after the doctrine of legislative ascendancy was widely discredited during the "critical period" (1781-1788) did the people gain the right to elect the governor by direct vote. Today a number of state constitutions permit voters to elect state judges as well.

The Framers of the U. S. Constitution looked on the principle of representation as an essential feature of a just and enduring republic, particularly an "extended," federal republic like the United States. Yet prior to the adoption of the Seventeenth Amendment (1913), the only federal officials directly chosen by the electorate were members of the House of Representatives. For various and weighty reasons, the men in Philadelphia settled on *indirect* modes of election for the senate, presidency, and federal judiciary. Whether or not such measures compromised the principle of representation remains a matter of debate. It bears considering, however, that the Framers were not beholden to the *majoritarian* principle. This is particularly evident in the system of checks and balances they created (e.g., bicameralism, veto, judicial review), and in the provisions for amending the Constitution (i.e., a super-majority in Congress and among the states). Hence, with regard to the national government, the Framers created a special kind of republic, one largely based on the principle of *indirect* and *non-majoritarian* representation. The apparent inconsistency between such "representation" and the principle of popular sovereignty has long been a curious anomaly of the American regime.

It has been observed that Machiavelli "was not interested in representative government . . ."[30] This judgment appears to stem from the Florentine's endorsement of the Roman Republic, where the "will of the people" was directly expressed in popular assemblies. Notwithstanding the practical checks on "direct democracy" in republican Rome, the plebeians were also represented by magistrates, the most important of which (consuls and tribunes) were popularly elected. Furthermore, Machiavelli viewed the practice of submitting proposals to the main assembly for an up or down vote far from ideal as a method of legislating.[31] With these considerations in mind, it is fair to say that Machiavelli *qua* republican was committed to the principle of representation. As such, he appears to place more faith in the wisdom of the people in their capacity to select capable "rulers" than many of the Framers did.[32] In any event, the supposition that Machiavelli was uninterested in the principle of representation is clearly refuted by the following passage in the *Discourses*.

> For if . . . two successive good and valorous princes are sufficient to
> conquer the world, as was the case with Philip of Macedon and Alexander
> the Great, a republic should be able to do still more, having the power to
> elect not only two successions, but an infinite number of the most
> competent and virtuous rulers one after the other; and this system of
> electing a succession of virtuous men should ever be the established
> practice of every republic. (*D*, I:20)

In suggesting that the *popolo* will consistently elect "the most competent and virtuous rulers" (*ma infiniti principi virtuosissimi*), Machiavelli
hastens to add a vital proviso: first, the electorate must be adequately
informed about the qualifications of the candidates, and second, the people
as a whole must be relatively free of "corruption." Assuming the presence
of the one and the absence of the other, he asserts that citizens will rarely
err in their choice of representatives. Machiavelli's faith in "the free
suffrages of the people" is particularly apparent in his remarks on the relative merit of popular election vs. executive appointment. In exploring this
question, Machiavelli concludes that in a healthy republic "[t]he people
. . . are influenced in the choice of their magistrates by the best evidence
(*cantrassegni*) they can obtain of the qualifications of candidates, and are
less liable to error than princes when equally counseled." (*D*, III:34) In
fine, "the people show more wisdom in their selection [of officials] than
princes."

From such passages it is evident that in *theory* Machiavelli embraced
the principle of direct election to a greater degree than the Framers did in
practice. Yet it is fair to assume that in a less than virtuous republic, he
would have accepted the need for indirect methods of election and non-
majoritarian modes of representation.[33] This assumption is born out by the
relevant provisions of his proposed constitution for the faction-rent Florence. For instance, Machiavelli's proposed assembly is to be filled on the
basis of popular election, whereas all other officials are to be selected by
appointment and indirect election. (*GF*) In practice, then, Machiavelli was
much closer to the Framers on the matter of representation than some of his
expositors have suggested.

12. *Liberty and Property* Order and stability are goals common to all
forms of government. Personal liberty (including the right to participate in
public affairs) and the secure enjoyment of private property, however, are
hallmarks of republicanism. Indeed, for the vast majority of Americans
these constitute (along with *justice*) the ultimate *ends* of government, to
which all other features of a republican order (e.g., separation of powers,
checks and balances) are simply the *means*. For eighteenth-century

Americans, *liberty* meant immunity from arbitrary government and the free exercise of man's natural and legal rights. The Founders endeavored to secure such freedom by creating a limited government under constitutions which enumerated the legitimate powers of the state, and incorporated specific guarantees (viz., bills of rights) for the protection of personal liberty.

While Jefferson spoke of the "pursuit of happiness" where Locke had spoken of property or "estate," most of the Founders looked upon private property as a "natural" right, the protection of which was among government's *raison d'être*. Some, like John Adams, believed that private property should be considered "as sacred as the laws of God." All agreed, however, that property rights were no less vital to liberty than freedom of conscience, jury trial, and frequent elections. "Property," wrote Adams, "is surely a right of mankind as really as liberty."[34]

It is not surprising, then, that much of the impetus for the Federal Convention stemmed from the threat to property rights, whether in the form of debt relief, stay laws, trade wars, or open insurrection. To met these threats (and prevent their recurrence) the Framers granted the federal government a monopoly on the coinage of money, prohibited the states from "impairing the obligation of contracts," and forbade the latter from taxing goods which crossed their borders. These provisions, directly and indirectly, prevented the *states* from infringing on the property rights of their residents. Restrictions on tariffs and taxation, as well as the due process and eminent domain clauses in the Fifth Amendment, helped protect these rights against encroachments by the *federal* government. In conjunction, such measures placed property rights on a par with the other rights and liberties Americans had fought to preserve.

Historians of political ideas are fond of reminding readers that those who wrote in the past did not always annex the same meaning to words subsequently employed by others. In the present case this warning is well-taken, for given the considerable extension of the concept of liberty in America, it is unlikely that Machiavelli meant precisely the same thing as the Founders did.[35] Complicating the matter is the fact that the Florentine was less interested in defining liberty than in suggesting how it can be maintained. It is clear, however, that, like the Founders, he viewed *libertà* as the chief end of a republic. Equally apparent is his conviction that the defense of freedom requires specific legal and constitutional provisions.

All the legislators that have given wise constitutions to republics have deemed it an essential precaution to establish a guard and protection to liberty (*è stato constituire una guardia alla libertà*); and accordingly as this was more or less wisely placed, liberty endured a greater and less length of time. (*D*, I:5)

Such reflections suggest that Machiavelli would not have been averse to something resembling a bill of rights on the American pattern. He does not, however, indicate precisely what would be included therein. Given his emphasis on the need for an "official" civic religion, it is safe to assume that a Machiavellian bill of rights would not contain a prohibition on religious establishments or a blanket grant of religious freedom. Neither would it likely contain an unqualified guarantee of freedom of speech and the press.[36] Yet given the Florentine's belief that citizens should be at liberty to make recommendations regarding matters of state, as well as formally accuse public officials, such restrictions on speech would not likely have been excessive by eighteenth-century standards. In fact, the only forms of expression he specifies as punishable are defamation and sedition (*D*, I:7, I:8), which have never been protected by the First Amendment. Moreover, there is nothing in Machiavelli's republican writings to suggest that he would object to most of the additional rights and liberties contained in the Constitution's first eight amendments. On the contrary, there are good reasons for suspecting that the Florentine would have strongly supported such provisions as equal protection under law, due process of law, as well as the rights of the accused.

On the subject of property, Machiavelli has little to say, but it may be reasonably inferred that he recognized the protection of private property as an essential feature of good government. For example, in his plan for reconstituting the Florentine government, he notes that under an earlier regime the Signoria (head of state) had "too much power, being able to dispose without appeal of the life and property (*roba*) of the citizens." (*GF*) In the same work, he laments the ill-effects of unbridled factionalism; viz., "riot" (*tumultuario*), "plunder" (*preda*), "exiles" (*esilj*), and "extortion" (*estorsioni*). In a more positive vein, Machiavelli notes that among "the advantages that result to the mass of the people from a free government" is the ability "to freely enjoy one's own [possessions] without apprehension" (*D*, I:16) Perhaps the most emphatic defense of property appears (ironically) in *The Prince*, where Machiavelli declares that "above all a prince must abstain from the property of others." (*Prince*, XVII) If this is his advice to an autocrat, can there be any doubt about the *republican* Machiavelli's commitment to property rights?

III. Additional Areas of Convergence

The foregoing comparison has revealed a series of notable parallels between the tenets of American republicanism and the republican Machiavelli. In conjunction these parallels demonstrate the impressive degree to which the Florentine *anticipated* the core principles of the American Founding. Yet the similarities do not end here, for a review of the remaining aspects of Machiavelli's republican teaching reveals at least four additional points of convergence which strengthen our conclusion.

13. *Human Nature and Civic Virtue* It is a common observation that all theories of politics are, explicitly or implicitly, based on a conception of human nature. "But what is government itself," Madison asks in *Federalist* No. 51, "but the greatest of all reflections on human nature?" He could assume an affirmative answer because, like his Enlightenment contemporaries, Madison believed that the essential features of man's nature were universal and fixed. When an Antifederalist noted that, "[t]he same passions and prejudices govern all men," he was not attempting to distinguish himself from the Federalists, but spoke for the vast majority of articulate Americans.[37] Indeed, it was this "fact," more than any other, that led men in the eighteenth century to confidently speak of the "science of politics."

The link between human nature and government is particularly clear in the thought of Alexander Hamilton, who at the Federal Convention observed that, "[t]he science of policy is the knowledge of human nature."[38] John Jay, the third author of *The Federalist*, also recognized that government must be "adapted to the actual state of human nature."[39] And while the specific political *implications* of man's basic nature remained a matter of debate, in America it was necessary to assume that men possessed the capacity for self-government in one form or another. This assumption implied that under the right conditions (viz., those which prevailed in America) men could develop sufficient virtue, public-spiritedness, and self-restraint to provide *security* and sustain *liberty*, thus satisfying the perennial desires of human nature.

Before and during the conflict with Great Britain, Americans tended to view themselves as socially distinct from and morally superior to the peoples of Europe. Politically speaking this implied that Americans were uniquely capable of establishing and sustaining virtuous, self-governing polities. Such a flattering conception of *homo Americanus* underwent a noticeable shift during the "critical period," as the spirit of nationalism and shared burdens gave way to the forces of local interest and individual gain. As George Washington ruefully observed in the wake of Shays' Rebellion, "We have, probably, had too good an opinion of human nature in forming our confederation."[40] At the same time John Jay wrote to Jefferson that, "there is reason to fear that too much has been expected from the virtue and good sense of the people."[41] Even earlier Hamilton, ever in the vanguard, observed that it was foolish to think that Americans were "wiser, or better than other men."[42]

Such admissions not only confirmed the bankruptcy of the Articles of Confederation, but questioned the viability of republicanism itself. Was not "public virtue" -- the regular subordination of narrow, private, local interests to the broader public good -- "the only foundation of republics"?[43] The events of the "critical period" had persuaded the delegates who gathered in Philadelphia that civic virtue could not be relied upon as the sole support of republicanism in America. Accordingly, they understood their task in terms of establishing a government that could secure order, property, and liberty without an *undue* reliance upon the mutual goodwill and cooperation of the people or the individual states. Succeeding in this endeavor, the Convention ultimately vindicated the cause of republicanism, in America and around the world. In the process, the emphasis on civic virtue as the lodestar of "classical" republicanism was largely eclipsed by the "liberal" notion of self-interest as the basis of society and politics.[44] The austere, enlightened patriot, the Framers suggested, was the exception rather than the rule, and could not be relied upon to sustain the "blessings of liberty." Moreover, it was simply unrealistic, even dangerous to expect that civic virtue (in the neo-classical sense) could thrive in a modern commercial republic such as the United States. If self-interest and acquisitiveness are inherent in man, a market society only encouraged these impulses. Under such circumstances, one might (as Hamilton observed) "preach till we are tired of the theme, the necessity of disinterestedness in republics, without making a single proselyte."[45]

This is not to suggest that the Framers considered civic virtue in the *general sense* irrelevant for a modern commercial republic. While it may be "a just *political* axiom" to assume the worst about men in *constructing* a polity, in its regular *functioning* it was also necessary to assume that the people and its representatives possessed sufficient virtue and good sense to sustain republican institutions. As Hamilton noted, "[t]he supposition of universal venality in human nature is little less an error in political reasoning than the supposition of universal rectitude." (*Federalist* No. 76) Indeed, a preference for "popular" government implied that, on balance, the good in man outweighs the bad: "Republican government," Madison observes, "presupposes the existence of these [virtuous] qualities in a higher degree than any other form." (*Federalist* No. 55) It is therefore misleading to suggest (as Wood has) that "the Federalists hoped to create an entirely new and original sort of republican government -- a republic which did not require a virtuous people for its sustenance."[46] As Madison bluntly informed the Virginia Ratifying Convention, if the electorate is devoid of sufficient "virtue and intelligence to select men of virtue and wisdom," "[n]o theoretical checks, no form of government, can render us secure."[47] Hence, while the "auxiliary precautions" built into the Constitution made it more difficult to subvert or disregard the broader public interest, it remained (as Hamilton later wrote) "essentially true that virtue or morality is a main and necessary spring of popular or republican Governments."[48]

When Hamilton suggested that "in contriving any system of government, and fixing the several checks and controls of the constitution, *every man* ought to be supposed a *knave*," he was citing the Scottish philosopher David Hume.[49] For his part, Hume had borrowed the thought directly from Machiavelli, who in the *Discourses* observes that "whoever desires to found a state and give it laws, must start with assuming that all men are bad and ever ready to display their vicious nature whenever they have occasion for it." (*D*, I:3) Machiavelli also anticipated Hume and the Founders in claiming that "all peoples are and ever have been animated by the same desires and passions . . ." (*D*, I:39) Indeed, it was just this insight that convinced the Florentine of the possibility of a prescriptive "science" of politics.[50] For if men have always been essentially the same, "it is easy by diligent study of the past to foresee what is likely to happen in the future," and thereby take appropriate action based on "the similarity of the events." (*D*, I:39) John Jay's endorsement of the principle that, "what has so often happened, would under similar circumstances happen" (*Federalist* No. 4), would certainly have gained Machiavelli's approval.

If there is a difference between Machiavelli and the Founders on the subject of human nature it is simply one of emphasis: in short, the Florentine appears less charitable and more cynical in his views. Both purport to take "human nature as it is, without flattering its virtues or exaggerating its vices" (*Federalist* No. 76), but Machiavelli tends to emphasize "the baseness of man" (*D*, II:2), believing as he does, that "mankind . . . [is] more prone to evil than to good." (*D*, I:9) Conversely, Machiavelli's cynicism is apparent in his rather patronizing view of "the great majority of mankind" who are "satisfied with appearances as if they were realities." (*D*, I:25) He recommends, for example, that the reforming legislator "retain the semblance of old forms" in order to avoid stirring the ire of the credulous masses.[51]

In truth, the view of human nature expressed by the authors of *The Federalist* is only slightly more sanguine. Hamilton, in particular, tends to underscore the "depravity of human nature" (*Federalist* No. 78), and recognizes *pace* Machiavelli that "[m]ankind are much led by sounds and appearances."[52] What allowed both men to reconcile such views with a commitment to republican government was a common belief in (1) the efficacy of institutional restraints, (2) the presence of a modicum of virtue among the masses, and (3) the existence and influence of "a few choice spirits, who may act from more worthy motives."[53] "[A]uxiliary precautions," in conjunction with that "portion of virtue and honor among mankind," could thus supply "a reasonable foundation of confidence" in the viability of popular government. (*Federalist* Nos. 51, 76)

Essentially the Florentine and the Founders were at one regarding the uniformity of human nature, its basic features, and its vital relevance for the legislator and statesman. With due qualification the same may be said in regard to their respective views on "civic virtue." (Machiavelli has long been recognized as a major figure in the "civic virtue" tradition and its revival in modern Europe.) Inspired by the *antica virtù* of the classical world (especially *virtù Romana*), Machiavelli made considerations of civic character central to his prescriptions for a viable republic. As "good laws" are largely a function of "good habits," he placed a premium on measures (viz., education, military service) designed to foster and sustain such habits. In this sense, civic virtue is intrinsic to self-government; a proposition bluntly confirmed by "the difficulty or impossibility of maintaining liberty in a republic that has become corrupt . . ." (*D*, I:18)

The Founders were not, of course, of one mind on the relation between "civic virtue" and "republican" government. Moreover, there was a general shift in opinion regarding the indispensability of civic virtue in the years following independence. Hence, if Machiavelli is taken to stand for "civic virtue" in its classical sense (which underscored austerity, patriotism, altruism, and participation in governing), his imprint will be seen most readily in the early state constitutions and among the Antifederalists. The constitutions of New Hampshire, North Carolina, Pennsylvania, and Virginia, for example, were unanimous in contending that "no free government, or the blessings of liberty, can be preserved to any people but by a firm adherence to justice, moderation, temperance, frugality, and virtue." More than a decade later, many Antifederalists continued to endorse this credo, and attacked the Constitution and its supporters for eschewing religion and morality as the basis of self-government. On the other hand, if the focus is on Machiavelli's concern with institutional restraints, the clash of interests, and the necessity of "superior" leadership, his civic philosophy appears to partake more of the Federalist persuasion. Such a dual application stems from the fact that the Florentine's political theory is a mixture of "classical" and "modern" elements, making it possible to find Machiavelli's stamp in both Federalist and Antifederalist camps.

14. **Faction** Since the appearance of Charles Beard's "economic" critique of the Constitution, the discussion of faction in *Federalist* No. 10 has been widely accepted as the key to understanding the political theory of the Framers. History and experience had convinced James Madison that

faction was the greatest threat to popular government, the survival of which hinged on devising a way to "break and control" its "violence." Madison was particularly concerned with *majority* faction, and its tendency "to sacrifice to its ruling passion or interest, both the public good and the rights of other citizens." In considering how to resist "the superior force of an interested and overbearing majority," Madison raised the possibility of removing the *causes* of faction. Admittedly, this entailed the extinction of liberty, a remedy "worse than the disease." Faction is therefore inevitable in a free society, and the only "cure" consistent with popular government requires "controlling its effects." Indeed, doing so constitutes the chief function of popular government.

> The regulation of these various and interfering interests forms the principal task of modern Legislation, and involves the spirit of party and faction in the necessary and ordinary operations of Government. (*Federalist* No. 10)

For Madison and the Framers, regulating the baneful effects of faction involved the following measures: (1) maintaining the principle of representation in place of direct democracy, (2) extending the public sphere over a large territory, and (3) dividing sovereignty between national and state authorities. In combination, these features of the American polity promised to provide "a Republican remedy for the diseases most incident to Republican Government."

The notion that social conflict was not merely inevitable, but potentially conducive to the well-being of a republic, is among the most novel of Machiavelli's political doctrines.[54] Like Madison, Machiavelli identifies faction as the peculiar bane of popular government: in fine, "factions cause their ruin." (*D*, I:7) Similarly, Madison agrees that "the latent causes of faction are . . . sown in the nature of man," and that "the most common and durable source of factions, has been the various and unequal distribution of property." (*Federalist* No. 10) The former position is clear from Machiavelli's remarks on human nature; the latter from his characterization of "the nobles" (*nobili*) and "the people" (*plebe*), "those who possess" and "those who have neither birth nor wealth." (*D*, I:5) The most striking feature of his remarks on faction, however, involves an ostensible contradiction. On one hand, he maintains that "factions . . . are the ruin of government" (*GF*), yet he also claims that "all the laws that are favorable to liberty result from the opposition" (*disunione*) between the *grandi* and the *popolo*. (*D*, I:4)[55] Sensing the apparent inconsistency, Machiavelli notes elsewhere that "some divisions (*divisioni*) harm republics and some divisions benefit them." (*HF*, VII:1) This qualification would appear to turn on a distinction between a "party" and a "faction." The former operates within the law and is animated by a sense of the public good, while the latter (to use Madison's language) is "united and actuated by some common impulse of passion, or of interest, adverse to the rights of other citizens, or to the permanent and aggregate interests of the community." (*Federalist* No. 10)

While Machiavelli's use of "faction" is ultimately ambivalent, he appears to have some preference for the term "parties" (*parti*) when referring to the positive results which "spring from [the] agitations" (*tumulti*) of "the people" and "the nobles." (*D*, I:4) Conversely, "faction" (*sette*) is typically associated with "the ruin of government." Further support for this reading appears in the Florentine's observation that, while "the founder of a republic cannot provide that there will be no enmities (*nimicizie*) within it, he needs at least to provide that there will be no factions" (*sette*). (*HF*, VII:1) If this means that no *parti* or *sette* should be allowed to *prevail*, we have the seeds of Madison's famous analysis of faction in the pages of Machiavelli. Moreover, if Madison can be read to suggest that the public good is indirectly served by the clash of private interests, we have further grounds for identifying the Florentine as the grandfather of pluralism and interest group politics.[56]

No account of Machiavelli's remarks on faction would be complete without noting that the issue of whether divisions within the body politic are salutary or poisonous depends *au fond* on the character of the people.[57]

> . . . we may draw the conclusion that where the mass of the people is
> sound, disturbances and tumults (*tumilti ed altri scandoli*) do no serious
> harm; but where corruption (*corrotta*) has penetrated the people, the best
> laws are of no avail. (*D*, I:17)

Here we find what appears to be the main difference between Madison and Machiavelli on faction. The Virginian acknowledges the truism that liberty and self-government require a degree of virtue among the people; "but experience has taught mankind the necessity of auxiliary precautions." (*Federalist* No. 51) It was just this concern that led Madison to tout the extended, federal republic as uniquely suited to diffusing "the pestilential breath of faction." (*Federalist* No. 81) Similarly, where virtue was lacking in the councils of government, the Constitution's provisions for separation of powers and checks and balances would "supply the defect of better motives." (*Federalist* No. 51)

As noted above, Machiavelli also recommends measures aimed at limiting power and checking its misuse; he does not, however, fully develop the concepts of representation or separation of powers, nor anticipate Madison's theory of the "extended republic" as antidotes to "the violence of faction." Under the spell of the Roman Republic, and conditioned by his Florentine heritage, Machiavelli desired a degree of participatory democracy in the context of the city-state. Working within this framework, he was not always clear on the subject of popular participation vs. representation. Nor did he advocate extending the sphere of government beyond the purlieus of the city as a means of diffusing the effects of faction. Such "omissions" notwithstanding, Machiavelli may be duly credited with identifying "faction" as the principal curse of popular governments, and suggesting the means of "controlling its effects."[58]

15. *Meritocracy* The provisions for equality under law in the American constitutions implied that individual merit should be the sole basis for public distinctions, including office holding. The first state constitutions did, however, place property qualifications (in some cases substantial ones) on office seekers. The Philadelphia Constitution contained no such restrictions; the only formal qualifications for holding federal office pertained to age, citizenship, and residency. In short, the Framers believed that the principle of merit should prevail under the new regime and were confident that men of talent and integrity would fill the ranks of the general government. (*Federalist*, Nos. 36, 57, 64)

Antifederalists often objected that it was naive to assume that men of virtue would prevail in the national councils; prudence demanded that additional safeguards be placed on "the rulers." Moreover, "brilliant talents" were not necessary in a republic, but "have for the most part been employed to mislead the honest, but unwary multitude, and draw them out of the open and plain paths of public virtue and public good."[59] Finally, even if these "natural aristocrats" did not deliberately betray the public trust, they could not be relied upon (due to a superiority which was admitted) to identify with the needs and interests of their less gifted constituents. Accordingly, many Antifederalists argued that the nation's representatives "should be a true picture of the people," and exhibit "a sameness as to residence and interests."[60]

Whatever the differences between the Federalists and their opponents over the nature of representation, both ultimately agreed that no artificial barriers should be placed on eligibility for public service. Among the finest expressions of the meritocratic principle appears in *The Federalist*, where Hamilton observes:

> There are strong minds in every walk of life that will rise superior to the disadvantages of situation, and will command the tribute due to their merit, not only from the classes to which they particularly belong, but

from the society in general. The door ought to be equally open to all. (*Federalist* No. 36)

A review of the *Discourses* reveals that Machiavelli was no less dedicated to the principle of merit than Hamilton. In rejecting the notion that only older men should be entrusted with power, the Florentine speaks approvingly of the Roman system, where "age never formed a necessary qualification for public office; merit [*virtù*] was the only consideration, whether found in young or old men." (*D*, I:60) And as for public honors and distinctions, "[t]he way to such honors should be open to every citizen, and suitable rewards should be established, that will be satisfactory and honorable to those who merit them." (*D*, III:28)

Machiavelli also addresses the issue of "talent" in a republic, and concurs with the Federalists on the necessity of selecting rulers who "possess most wisdom to discern, and most virtue to pursue, the common good of society." (*Federalist* No. 57) In his own words, "a republic that has no distinguished citizens (*cittadini riputati*) cannot be well-governed." (*D*, III:28) Yet like the Antifederalists, Machiavelli recognized that "it is often the great influence of such distinguished citizens that is the cause of states being reduced to servitude." His solution to this dilemma appears to fall somewhere between the system of checks and balances contained in the Constitution and the additional restraints on public officials (e.g., rotation, annual elections) advocated by Antifederalists. More to the point, Machiavelli embraced the principle of "careers open to talent" as a means of directing the energies and ambitions of men in a manner conducive to the public good. Like many of the Federalists, Machiavelli understood that species of man who, upon finding no opportunity to gain honor through public service, either lapse into despondency or pursue their thirst for distinction in illicit ways. Hence the Florentine would have strongly seconded Robert Livingston's observation that, "[t]he acquisition of abilities is hardly worth the trouble, unless one is to enjoy the satisfaction of employing them for the good of one's country."[61] "A well-regulated republic, therefore, should open the way to public honors to those who seek reputation by means that are conducive to the public good." (*D*, III:28)

16. ***Recurrence to First Principles*** Machiavelli's contention that a republic must periodically return to its "original principles" (*ridurre ai principii*) in order to preserve its health and security, is among the doctrines which had a *direct* impact on the American Founders. In the Florentine's thought, the notion of a recurrence to first principles is identified as the indispensable "remedy" for ailing republics. Accordingly, Machiavelli *qua* political

physician, prescribes "a return of the citizens to the original principles of the republic" as the singular antidote to the progressive decay incident to all regimes. (*D*, III:1)

> ... those are the best-constituted [political] bodies, and have the longest existence, which possess the intrinsic means of frequently renewing themselves, or such as obtain this renovation in consequence of some extrinsic accidents. And it is a truth clearer than light that, without such renovation, these bodies cannot continue to exist; and the means of renewing them is to bring them back to their original principles. (*D*, III:1)

The theme of corruption and renewal was transmitted to the colonies by such writers as the English reformers James Harrington (1611-1677) and Algernon Sidney (1623-1683), who adopted it directly from Machiavelli. "Demophilus" (a pseudonymous American patriot) approvingly quotes Sidney's dictum that "all human Constitutions are subject to corruption, and must perish, unless they are *timely renewed* by reducing them to their first principles."[62] Since Sidney and other widely-read "Opposition" writers cited Machiavelli as the source of this doctrine, it is certain that colonial readers were aware of its origin.[63] Indeed, as early as 1768 John Dickinson, in his influential *Letters from a Farmer*, drew directly on the Florentine's authority, informing his readers that "Machiavel employs a whole chapter in his discourses, to prove that a state, to be longed lived, must be frequently corrected, and reduced to its first principles."[64] Here the "state" in question is Great Britain, which was viewed by an increasing number of Americans as notably "corrupt" and in dire need of "reform." Indeed, long before the colonists declared their independence, such sentiments had become commonplace among whigs and republicans on both sides of the Atlantic.

George Mason provides a further example of Machiavelli's direct influence in this area. A revolutionary leader in Virginia and delegate to the Philadelphia Convention, Mason remarked in 1775 that, "it has been wisely observed by the deepest politician who ever put pen to paper [Machiavelli], that no institution can be long preserved, but by frequent recurrence to those maxims on which it was formed."[65] While few may have shared Mason's enthusiasm for the Florentine, the Machiavellian imprint is unmistakable. Like his neo-classical doctrine of "civic virtue," Machiavelli's belief that "a frequent recurrence to fundamental principles is absolutely necessary to preserve the blessings of liberty" found its way into a number of state constitutions.

In assessing the significance of this Machiavellian theme, Gerald Stourzh has written: "The era of the American Revolution and the framing of the Constitution witnessed the last glowing of the Renaissance tradition of political philosophy that regarded decay and corruption as the basic rule of historical change."[66] It is, however, Machiavelli's prescriptions for *renewal* that Stourzh identifies as "the source of two ideas of paramount significance for the intellectual outlook of the Founding Fathers." The first idea includes such formal measures as frequent elections, short legislative sessions, and the amendment process. These and other provisions were incorporated into the state and federal constitutions in order to (at least in part) avert corruption and abuses of power, on the one hand, and to reinvigorate the government on the other. The second idea entails the use of force or extra-legal methods as a means of restoring a commonwealth to its original principles. This idea appears in the Declaration of Independence, where Jefferson proclaims it not only a "right," but a "duty to throw off" the chains of oppressive government.

While Machiavelli does not employ the Lockean language of "rights" and "duties," he would have appreciated Jefferson's (and the colonists') willingness to resort to obstruction and arms in order to preserve liberty and self-government. Given the Florentine's emphasis on the need for an occasional "shock" to the system, he would have been equally pleased with Jefferson's famous response to Shays' Rebellion in 1787.

> God forbid that we should ever be 20 years without such a rebellion. . . .
> What signify a few lives lost in a century or two? The tree of liberty must
> be refreshed from time to time with the blood of patriots and tyrants.[67]

Jefferson did not, of course, endorse rebellion for its own sake, but like Machiavelli, recognized the utility of "a little rebellion now and then" as a means of redressing grievances, invigorating the body politic, and restoring a wayward commonwealth to its first principles.[68] Machiavelli does, however, suggest that in cases where the people are notably corrupt, only a single ruler with plenary authority can ever hope to restore virtue among the citizens. (*D*, I:25, III:1) He also suggests that in certain instances a return to first principles would be attended by more than just "a few lives lost," not to mention confiscations, exiles, and executions. (*D*, I:18) Yet in agreeing to the desirability of periodic popular outbursts followed by timely reforms, Jefferson and Machiavelli shared a common view regarding the dynamics of popular government and the maintenance of liberty.

IV. Conclusion

With the addition of the foregoing areas of convergence, our comparison between the leading tenets of the American Founders and the republicanism of Machiavelli is complete. While there are a few additional points of similarity (e.g., citizen army, use of history), these are less vital than the principles discussed above. As such, our review of these principles has established the presence of an undeniable kinship and remarkable affinity between the foundations of American republicanism and the republican Machiavelli.

I suspect, nevertheless, that some readers will find fault with this assessment and attribute my findings to superficial analysis and over-wrought comparisons.[69] In anticipation of this criticism, I concede that the emphasis here has been on similarities at the expense of differences. Yet in exploring the former, I have neither denied nor attempted to conceal the existence of the latter. In the interest of accuracy, however, it is necessary to acknowledge the presence of a few additional points of difference of a more fundamental kind. These are Machiavelli's (1) contention that a viable republic requires an official civic religion, (2) endorsement of dictatorship in times of national emergency, (3) belief that a republic's constitution must be the creation of a single hand, (4) emphasis on expansion and imperialism; and (5) suggestion that the citizens of a republic should be kept "poor" in order to remain virtuous.

Even in these areas it is possible to find a few parallels in the political literature of the Founding era; however most Americans were (1) hostile to religious establishments, (2) opposed to the concept of dictatorship, (3) suspicious of anything resembling a Mosaic legislator, (4) ambivalent or indifferent toward territorial expansion and conquest, and (5) intent of improving their economic condition.

It will also be acknowledged that at times I have built my comparisons on inference and supposition. In such cases I have informed the reader accordingly and qualified my conclusions. Finally, I admit to placing Machiavelli's republicanism in a generally favorable light. However, I have done so on the basis of his own words, which readily lend themselves to such a construction. Ultimately, it is the reader who must pass judgment on the soundness of my analysis and the persuasiveness of my findings. A fair verdict will give equal weight to both the spirit and letter of Machia-velli's republican writings. If my findings survive such scrutiny, perhaps the Antifederalist "Maryland Farmer" should receive part of the credit.

The greatest human discernment, ever concentrated in the mind of one man, was the portion of the celebrated Nicholas Machiavelli -- a name loaded with abuse by tyrants, flatters and the mushrooms of science, because he told the truth; because he was a republican and the friend of mankind in times of usurpation; or because, they have never read or do not understand his works.[70]

loaded with abuse by tyrants, flatters and the mushrooms of science, because he told the truth; because he was a republican and the friend of mankind in times of usurpation; or because, they have never read or do not understand his works.[70]

Notes

1. *The Ideological Origins of the American Revolution* (Cambridge, Mass., 1967); *The Creation of the American Republic, 1776-1788* (New York, 1969).

2. Wood, *American Republic*, 29.

3. It should be noted that Gerald Strourzh, in a work published just a year after Gordon Wood's landmark study, discussed the link between Machiavelli and the Founders at some length. While Wood had argued that the shift in "ideology" which resulted in the Federal Constitution marked "an end of the classical conception of politics" (*American Republic*, 606), it was Stourzh who explicitly noted that "[t]he era of the American Revolution and the framing of the Constitution witnessed the last glowing of the Renaissance tradition of political philosophy . . ." *Alexander Hamilton and the Idea of Republican Government* (Stanford, 1970), 35-36. In this observance, Stourzh appears to have anticipated Pocock's "Machiavellian moment."

4. Here Pocock built on Zera S. Fink's seminal study *The Classical Republicans: An Essay in the Recovery of a Pattern of Thought in Seventeenth-Century England* (Evanston, Ill., 1945). In the course of her discussion, Fink documents the seminal influence of the "republican" Machiavelli on such figures as James Harrington, John Milton, and Algernon Sydney, authors who were widely read by eighteenth-century Americans.

5. "The interpretation put forward here," writes Pocock, "stresses Machiavelli at the expense of Locke. . . . It suggests that the foundation of independent America was seen, and stated, as taking place at a Machiavellian . . . moment, at which the fragility of the experiment, and the ambiguity of the republic's position in secular time, was more vividly appreciated than it could have been from a Lockean perspective." *The Machiavellian Moment: Florentine Political Thought and the Atlantic Republican Tradition* (Princeton, 1975), 545.

6. The foremost critic of the traditional approach to the history of political thought has been Quentin Skinner. In contrast to the text-centered analysis of most political theorists, Professor Skinner and his "Cambridge School" colleagues have pioneered an essentially historical approach to the study of political ideas, emphasizing such factors as social context, linguistic conventions, conceptual paradigms, and authorial intent. Skinner's methodological essays (and some critical responses) have been collected in *Meaning and Context: Quentin Skinner and his Critics* (Princeton, 1988).

7. See *The Federal and State Constitutions, Colonial Charters, and Other Organic Laws . . .*, 7 vols., ed., Francis N. Thorpe (Washington, D. C., 1909).

8. It appears that Machiavelli's doctrine of popular sovereignty owes as much to prudential considerations as principled or theoretical ones. As Sheldon Wolin writes, "[h]e grasped the fact that popular consent represented a form of social power which, if properly exploited, reduced the amount of violence directed at society as a whole. One reason for the superiority of the republican system consisted in its being maintained by the force of the populace, rather than by force over the populace." *Politics and Vision: Continuity and Innovation in Western Political Theory* (Boston, 1960), 223.

9. In its pure form, legal positivism holds that the sole standard of moral and political "right" (including obligation) is represented by "positive" or man-made law. In contrast, "natural law" theory holds that there is a superior or "higher" standard to which positive law must conform if it is to be legitimate and morally binding. Yet because Machiavelli fails to provide a doctrine of political right *per se*, it is probably more accurate to call him a positivist by default. As John Plamenatz writes, "I would be tempted to call [Machiavelli] a positivist, if that word were not already associated with the theories of Comte and his disciples. He does not consciously put forward any ultimate moral principles; he takes for granted that men want security and need strong government, and he tells them how to get what they want and need . . ." *Man and Society, Political and Social Theory: Machiavelli through Rousseau* (New York, 1963), 7.

10. *Second Treatise of Government* [1690] ed., C. B. Macpherson (Indianapolis, 1980)

11. As Nicolai Rubinstein notes, Machiavelli exhibits an "apparent lack of interest in some of the basic questions of classical and scholastic political philosophy -- such as the role of justice in the state, the nature of law, the limits of political obligation, and the relationship between the temporal and the spiritual power." "Italian Political Thought, 1450-1530," in *Cambridge History of Political Thought, 1450-1700*, ed., J. H. Burns (Cambridge, Eng., 1991), 47. I concur with Rubinstein that such omissions are largely explained by Machiavelli's "historical and empirical method of political enquiry . . ."

12. Machiavelli's "concept of law," writes Rubinstein, ". . . is unreservedly positivist: the validity of human law depends in no way upon its conformity to a higher law." "Italian Political Thought," 49. While this is essentially correct, Machiavelli's silence on the issue of natural law should not be read as a blunt affirmation of positivism. Moreover, on occasion Machiavelli indicates that he *does* recognize a higher law than mere prescription. For example, he refers to Philip of Macedon's methods of forced relocation as "the cruelest, and the enemies of every way of life, not only Christian but the human; and any man ought to flee them . . ." (*D*, I:26). On the basis of such examples, Sebastian de Garzia concludes that Machiavelli

embraced natural and divine law; for instance, he believed "the norms that tyrants break are natural, human, and divine." *Machiavelli in Hell* (New York, 1989), 85-86.

13. As A. J. Parel has argued, this does not imply that Machiavelli "had no use for justice," as some commentators have maintained. Admittedly, "justice as such does not constitute a focal point of his political thought," and there is "no evidence in his major writings which supports the view that justice has a natural basis in practical reason . . ." Yet the Florentine secretary "came to learn early in his career the very simple lesson that without the practice of some form of justice, no one could be a good administrator; legal justice and administrative justice constituted the backbone of any good government." "Machiavelli's Notions of Justice: Text and Analysis," *Political Theory*, 18 (1990), 536, 530, 536, 531. As Parel's analysis suggests, Machiavelli's republican commitments argue strongly against a strictly amoral or immoral reading of the Florentine *á la* Leo Strauss in *Thoughts on Machiavelli* (Chicago, 1958).

14. In an age when free cities and republics where the exception and principalities and monarchies the rule, Machiavelli was on solid ground in this assessment. Moreover, he believed that a regime should reflect the fundamental disposition and experience of the people, particularly in regard to the principle of equality. Hence his dictum: "Let republics . . . be established where equality exists, and on the contrary, principalities where great inequality prevails." (*D*, I:55, I:49; *GF*) While the Founders did not adopt this precise formula, they agreed that republican government was unsustainable under certain conditions.

15. As Bernard Crick writes, "kings to Machiavelli are those princes who abide by the existing laws of the state: hence there is no incompatibility between having a king and being a republic, although if there never have been free institutions and the traditional laws are those of any autocracy, than the king can be the strongest and most stable kind of prince or ruler." "Introduction," in *The Discourses*, trans. Leslie J. Walker (New York, 1970), 20n. Yet even in the latter case, Machiavelli "is sometimes (though not consistently) willing to believe that the maintenance of popular control may be compatible with a monarchical form of government." Quentin Skinner, *Machiavelli* (Oxford, 1981), 52. Moreover, Machiavelli distinguishes between a despotism or "absolute government" (*potestà assoluta*) and a kingdom or "monarchy" (*regno*). (*D*, I:25, I:58)

16. Providing a formal system of "legal accusations" against unlawful or seditious activities, including punishments for canards and "calumnies" is a critical feature of Machiavelli's republicanism. "Such a system has two very marked advantages for a republic. The first is that the apprehension of being accused prevents the citizens from attempting anything against the state" -- hardly a idle concern in Renaissance Italy. "The other is that it affords a way for those evil dispositions that arise in one way or another against some citizen to vent themselves . . ." (*D*, I:7) This feature of the Florentine's republicanism is cited with approval by the authors of

Cato's Letters, an influential English "Opposition" tract reprinted in America in the 1720s. In Letter No. 32, "Cato" observes: "Machiavel says, Calumny is pernicious, but accusation beneficial, to a state; . . ." *Cato's Letters*, 2 vols., ed., Ronald Hamowy (Indianapolis, 1995). Widely read in the colonies, "Cato's Letters" is generally recognized as "one of the most important avenues or bridges by which Machiavelli's thought was transmitted to America." Thomas L. Pangle, *The Spirit of Modern Republicanism: The Moral Vision of the American Founders and the Philosophy of Locke* (Chicago, 1988), 30.

17. Quoted in Wood, *American Republic*, vii.

18. Gisela Bock, "Civil Discord in Machiavelli's *Istorie Fiorentine*," in *Machiavelli and Republicanism* (Cambridge, Eng., 1990), 189.

19. *Leviathan* [1651], ed., Michael Oakeshott (New York, 1962), II:21.

20. David Wootton notes that while Machiavelli "occasionally uses the word *constituzione*, his use is not in a comprehensive sense; in the *Discourses* he does not use the word *regime*, which would call to mind *politeia*, the Greek word for 'constitution' that was extensively defined by Aristotle." "Introduction," in *Niccolò Machiavelli: Selected Political Writings* (Indianapolis, 1994), xxx. J. H. Whitfield, who underscores Machiavelli's commitment to constitutional government, observes that *ordini* and its cognates (*modi, leggi, constituere*, and *constituzioni*) appear 761 times in the *Discourses*, 80 times in *The Prince*, 125 times in *History of Florence*, 76 times in the *Art of War*, and 36 times in *A Discourse on Remodeling the Government of Florence*. See *Discourses on Machiavelli* (Cambridge, Eng., 1969), 141-163.

21. On the surface it may appear odd that while Machiavelli approved of the *parlements*, he also supported the French kings' efforts to increase royal power at the expense of the nobles, and showed little sympathy for the States-General, the nearest thing in France to a popular assembly. (*Prince*, XIX) Yet as Plamenatz observes, "the *parlements*, while they restrained monarchy, sympathized with its endeavors to make France law-abiding, united, and strong, whereas the States-General were dominated by the nobles and the priests, who cared more for the privileges of their class or order than for the good of the State." *Man and Society*, 40.

22. Thomas Jefferson, *Notes on the State of Virginia*, ed., H. A. Washington (New York, 1964), 113.

23. John Adams, who among the Founders was best-acquainted with Machiavelli, faulted him on this very point. Specifically, he accused the Florentine of failing to appreciate the necessity of creating "a separate executive, with power to defend itself" as a means of remedying the "fatal effects of dissensions between the nobles and the commons." Yet in making this claim (i.e., that the idea of a single

executive with a legislative veto "seems never to have entered his thoughts"), Adams appears to have overlooked a feature in Machiavelli's proposed "constitution" for Florence, viz., a single Provost authorized to "veto" (*impedire*) decisions reached by the Signoria, until the matter could be appealed to a council, which might further delay the issue. Adams quoted in C. Bradley Thomas, "John Adams' Machiavellian Moment," *Review of Politics*, 53 (1995), 412.

24. *State of Virginia*, 113.

25. See Frank W. Walbank, "Polybius and the Roman State," in *Perspectives in Political Philosophy: Thucydides to Machiavelli*, ed., James V. Downton and David K. Hart (New York, 1971), 181-199

26. Crick's contention that the *Discourses* contains only "a hint of checks and balances" is somewhat of an understatement. "Introduction," 32. Moreover, Machiavelli's reform plan for Florence (as Sydney Anglo observes) contains "an elaborate system of checks and balances, all devised in the name of freedom." *Machiavelli: A Dissection* (London, 1969), 161.

27. George Mason, James Wilson, and Edmund Randolph, in *The Records of the Federal Convention of 1787*, 4 vols., ed., Max Farrand (New Haven, 1966), I:48, II:522, I:66.

28. For a discussion of the Aristotelian-cum-Polybian elements in Machiavelli's conception of the mixed regime, see John P. McCormick, "Addressing the Political Exception: Machiavelli's 'Accidents' and the Mixed Regime," *American Political Science Review*, 87 (1993), 888-900.

29. As Crick observes, the "mixture" envisaged by Machiavelli "is not a static matter of checks and balances, but a dynamic blending of three elements that are needed in different proportions at different times; and a republic contains, indeed nurtures, all the three elements, whereas a principality has to suppress all but one." "Introduction," 29.

30. Plamenatz, *Man and Society*, 43.

31. As Machiavelli writes, "[t]hose who have been present at any deliberative assemblies of men will have observed how erroneous their opinions often are; and in fact, unless they are directed by superior men, they are apt to be contrary to all reason." (*D*, II:22) Compare this with Madison: "In all very numerous assemblies of whatever characters composed, passion never fails to wrest the scepter from reason. Had every Athenian citizen been a Socrates, ever Athenian assembly would still have been a mob." *Federalist* No. 55. Elsewhere, Machiavelli tacitly criticizes the plebiscitary aspect of the Roman Republic, observing that "we cannot call that republic well-established in which things are done according to the will of one man yet are decided with the approval of many." (*GF*)

32. Even the "egalitarian" Jefferson held reservations regarding the ability of "the people" to elect capable leaders. As he wrote a friend, "I have ever observed that a choice by the people themselves is not generally distinguished for its wisdom." Jefferson to Edmund Pendleton (Aug. 26, 1776), in *The Papers of Thomas Jefferson*, ed., Julian P. Boyd (Princeton, 1950), I:503.

33. It should be noted that the Roman constitution embodied indirect modes of election (e.g., the appointment of senators by popularly elected consuls), as well as non-majoritarian features (e.g., the senate's normal control over the formulation of legislation; the right of a consul to veto measures introduced by his colleague). For a detailed account of the institutions of the Roman Republic, see Karl Lowenstein, *The Governance of Rome* (The Hague, 1973), 41-177.

34. *Defence of the Constitutions of the United States* (1787), in *The Founders' Constitution*, 5 vols., ed., Philip B. Kurland and Ralph Lerner (Chicago, 1987), I:591.

35. For a thorough treatment of Machiavelli's conception of "liberty," see Marcia L. Colish, "The Idea of Liberty In Machiavelli," *Journal of the History of Ideas* 32 (1971), 323-350.

36. "Freedom, as it was understood in Machiavelli's time," writes Plamenatz, "did not include liberty of conscience. Champions of freedom in his day were not much concerned to protect the rights of dissident minorities or individuals who rejected commonly received principles. . . . Yet Machiavelli had a high regard for personal dignity and independence." *Man and Society*, 37.

37. Melancton Smith, in *The Complete Anti-Federalist*, ed., Herbert J. Storing, 7 vols. (Chicago, 1981), 6.12.17.

38. Farrand, *Records*, I:378.

39. Jay to Jefferson (April 24, 1787), in *The Correspondence and Public Papers of John Jay, 1763-1826*, 4 vols., ed., Henry P. Johnston (New York, 1890-1893), III:245.

40. Washington to Jay (August 15, 1786), in *Correspondence*, III:208.

41. Jay to Jefferson (February 9, 1787), in *Correspondence*, III:232.

42. *The Continentalist* No. 3 (Aug. 9, 1781), in *The Papers of Alexander Hamilton*, 27 vols., ed., Harold C. Syrett (New York, 1961-1987), II:660.

43. John Adams to Mercy Warren (April 16, 1776), in Kurland and Lerner, *Founders' Constitution*, I:670.

44. As John Diggins has written, "[b]etween Machiavelli and Locke lies the dilemma of American politics. Classical political philosophy aims to discipline man's desires and raise him far above his vulgar wants; liberalism promises to realize desires and satisfy wants. The first is more noble, the second more attainable." *The Lost Soul of American Politics: Virtue, Self-Interest, and the Foundations of Liberalism* (New York, 1984), 16.

45. *The Continentalist* No. 6 (July 4, 1782), in *Papers of Alexander Hamilton*, III:103.

46. *American Republic*, 475.

47. *The Debates in the Several State Conventions on the Adoption of the Federal Constitution* . . ., 5 vols., ed., Jonathan Eliot, 2nd ed. (Philadelphia, 1876), III:536-537. Compare with Machiavelli: "But if the people had been corrupt, then there would have been no sufficient remedies found in Rome or elsewhere to maintain their liberty." (*D*, I:7)

48. Draft of Washington's "Farewell Address" (July 30, 1796), in *Papers of Alexander Hamilton*, XX:280.

49. *The Farmer Refuted* (February 23, 1775), in *Papers of Alexander Hamilton*, I:95.

50. Ernst Cassier has noted that "[w]hat Galileo gave in his *Dialogues*, and what Machiavelli gave in his *Prince* were really 'new sciences' . . . Just as Galileo's Dynamics became the foundation of our modern science of nature, so Machiavelli paved a new way to political science." *The Myth of the State* (New Haven, 1946), 130. See also Leonard Olschki, *Machiavelli the Scientist* (Berkeley, 1945).

51. This is precisely what an Antifederalist writer accused the Framers of doing: "they have continued the forms of the particular governments, and termed the whole a confederation of the United States, *pursuant to the sentiments of that profound but corrupt politician Machiavel*, who advises any one who would change the constitution of a state, to keep as much as possible to the old forms; for then the people seeing the same officers, the same formalities, courts of justice, and other outward appearances, are insensible of the alteration, and believe themselves in possession of their old government [emphasis added]." "Letters of Centinal," in Storing, *Complete Anti-Federalist*, 2.7.67.

52. Unaddressed Letter (Dec. 1779), in *Papers of Alexander Hamilton*, II:247.

53. Hamilton, in Farrand, *Records*, I:381. We have noted many of the institutional measures Machiavelli endorsed in the name of reconciling order and liberty. Given this emphasis, it is somewhat misleading to assert (as Quentin Skinner has) that Machiavelli, *contra* Hume and the Framers, exemplifies that tradition "which

stresses that it is not so much the machinery of government as the proper *spirit* of the rulers, the people and the laws which needs above all to be sustained." *Foundations of Modern Political Thought: The Renaissance* (Cambridge, Eng. 1978), 45. The notion that "civic virtue" is the sole support of Machiavelli's republican polity is simply not born out by his writings. He does, however (like the Framers), agree that a modicum of virtue among the *popolo* is required to sustain a republic (*D*, I:4, I:5, I:58), and that policy should be "directed by superior men" distinguished for their "respectability and virtue." (*D*, II:22, I:36)

54. Machiavelli's "astonishing contentions that discord can actually strengthen a state;" that "political conflict can be functional;" and that "[l]iberty itself . . . arises from conflicts," have been well-noted by his expositors. Crick, "Introduction," 34, 37, 35. Skinner, for example, observes that "Machiavelli's argument ran counter to the whole tradition of republican thought in Florence, a tradition in which the belief that faction constitutes the deadliest threat to civic liberty, had been emphasized since the end of the thirteenth century . . ." To suggest otherwise, "was to repudiate one of the most cherished assumptions of Florentine humanism." *Machiavelli*, 66.

55. Harvey Mansfield attempts to explain the apparent discrepancy in Machiavelli's theory of faction by arguing that "Machiavelli sees conflicts between factions [within a class] as destructive, while conflicts between classes are constructive." Furthermore, "Machiavelli . . . views conflicts that are founded in divergent economic interests and differing social statuses as inevitable, and indeed healthy. Where these conflicts result in a balance of power and a mixed constitution, something resembling the general good, *il bene commune*, will result, and selfish, short-sighted individuals will end up behaving like virtuous citizens." "Introduction," in *Discourses on Livy*, trans. Harvey C. Mansfield and Nathan Tarcov (Chicago, 1996), xxxii.

56. As Plamenatz writes, "at bottom, [Machiavelli's] conception [of faction] is not very different from ours. Freedom is preserved by a competition for power kept within bounds by respect for law, and also by a common loyalty to the State. This competition, so long as the law is respected, does not weaken the State but makes it stronger, because it requires vigilance, energy, and courage in the competitors." *Man and Society*, 39. See also David E. Ingersoll, "The Constant Prince: Private Interests and Public Goals in Machiavelli," *Western Political Quarterly*, 21 (1968), 588-596; and "Madison and Machiavelli: Perspectives on Political Stability," *Political Science Quarterly*, 85 (1970), 259-280. While Madison does not appear to have been directly influenced by Machiavelli, it is noteworthy that he included "The Works of Nicholas Machiavelli" in "a list of books to be imported for the use of the United States in Congress Assembled," which Madison compiled and presented to Congress in 1783. See "Report on Books for Congress," in *The Papers of James Madison*, ed., Robert A. Rutland (Chicago, 1975), VI:62-65, 86.

57. As Colish writes, "Machiavelli's distinction between the negative and positive effects of factionalism on liberty seems to rest on the question of whether the state in which factions operate is corrupt or uncorrupted." "Idea of Liberty ," 340.

58. In Skinner's words, Machiavelli's "solution" to the problem of social conflict and political instability "is to frame the laws relating to the constitution in such a way as to engineer a tensely-balanced equilibrium between these opposed social forces, one in which all the parties remain involved in the business of government, and each 'keeps watch over the other' in order to forestall both 'the rich man's arrogance' and 'the people's license'. As the rival groups jealously scrutinize each other for any signs of a move to take over supreme power, the resolution of the pressures thus engendered will mean that only those 'laws and institutions' which are 'conducive to public liberty' will actually be passed. Although motivated entirely by their selfish interest, the factions will thus be guided, as if by an invisible hand, to promote the public interest in all their legislative acts: 'all the laws made in favor of liberty' will 'result from their discord'." Yet just as the Framers believed that separation of powers and checks and balances were required to safeguard liberty but could not *in themselves* do so, Machiavelli "argue[s] that although a mixed constitution is necessary, it is by no means sufficient, to ensure that liberty is preserved." *Machiavelli*, 66-67. As noted above, what is also required is a modicum of "civic virtue" and public spiritedness on behalf of the governors and the governed.

59. "Federal Farmer" and "Friend of the Republic," in Storing, *Complete Anti-Federalist*, 2.8.158; 4.23.8.

60. Melancton Smith and "Federal Farmer," in Storing, *Complete Anti-Federalist*, 6.12.15; 2.8.158.

61. New York Ratifying Convention, in Eliot, *Debates*, II:293.

62. Quoted in Wood, *American Republic*, 34.

63. The aforementioned "Cato" informed his readers that "Machiavel tells us that no government can long subsist, but by recurring often to its first principles." Letter No. 16. Michael Lienesch has noted that the theme of corruption and renewal, which was "so crucial to creating the revolutionary strain in republicanism, was repeated by the radical Whig reformers from Harrington, Henry Neville, and Algernon Sidney, and . . . gained wide influence through the eighteenth-century libertarian tracts of John Trenchard and Thomas Gordon [aka "Cato"], who in the decades after 1688 called on their fellow republicans to rise up and recapture the liberties lost to scheming court politicians." *New Order of the Ages: Time, the Constitution, and the Making of Modern American Political Thought* (Princeton, 1988), 65.

64. John Dickinson, *Letters from a Farmer . . .*, Letter No. 11 (New York, 1903), 117.

65. Remarks on Annual Elections for the Fairfax Independent Company (c. April 17-26, 1775), in *The Papers of George Mason*, 3 vols., ed., Robert L. Rutland (Chapel Hill, 1970), I:229.

66. *Alexander Hamilton*, 35-36.

67. Jefferson to William Stephens Smith (Nov. 13, 1787), in *Papers of Thomas Jefferson* (Princeton, 1955), XII:356. Interestingly, while Jefferson put a two decade time-limit between popular outbursts, Machiavelli argued that "[i]t would be desirable . . . that not more than ten years should elapse" before such unrest expressed itself openly. (*D*, III:1)

68. See Paul A. Rahe, "Thomas Jefferson's Machiavellian Political Science," *Review of Politics*, 57 (1995), 450-481.

69. Mark Hulliung, for example, notes that Machiavelli's republican rhetoric of "liberty and constitutional order" has led many readers to assume that they are "in the presence of a kindred spirit, when nothing could be further from the truth." *Citizen Machiavelli* (Princeton, 1983), 220. While there are admittedly important *differences* between the republican Machiavelli and the republicanism of the Founders, Hulliung's suggestion that the *similarities* are superficial is unsustainable in light of the analysis presented here.

70. Storing, *Complete Anti-Federalist*, 5.1.81.

The Other Machiavelli

I. Man and State

Let no one, then, fear not to be able to accomplish what others have done, for all men . . . are born and live and die in the same way, and therefore resemble each other. (*D*, I:9)

It was a saying of ancient writers, that men afflict themselves in evil and become weary of the good, and that both these dispositions produce the same effects. For when men are no longer obliged to fight from necessity, they fight from ambition, which passion is so powerful in the hearts of men that it never leaves them, no mater to what height they may rise. The reason of this is that nature has created men so that they desire everything, but are unable to attain it; desire being thus always greater than the faculty of acquiring, discontent with what they have and dissatisfaction with themselves result from it. This causes the changes in their fortunes; for as some men desire to have more, while others fear to lose what they have, enmities and war are the consequences; and this brings about the ruin of one province and the elevation of another. (*D*, I:37)

[W]e should notice also how easily men are corrupted and become wicked, although originally good and well-educated. (*D*, I:42)

Men ever praise the olden time, and find fault with the present, though often without reason. They are such partisans of the past that they extol not only the times which they know only by the accounts left of them by historians, but having grown old, they also laud all they remember to have seen in their youth. Their opinion is generally erroneous in that respect, and I think the reasons which cause this illusion are various. The first I believe to be the fact that we never know the whole truth about the past, and very frequently writers conceal such events as would reflect disgrace upon their century, while they magnify and amplify those that lend luster to it. The majority of authors obey the fortune of conquerors to that degree that, by way of rendering their victories more glorious, they exaggerate not only the valiant deeds of the victor, but also of the vanquished; so that future generations of the countries of both will have cause to wonder at those men and times, and are obliged to praise and admire them to the utmost. Another reason is that men's hatreds generally spring from fear or envy. Now these two powerful reasons of hatred do not exist for us with regard to the past, which can no longer inspire either apprehension or envy. But it is very different with the affairs of the present, in which we ourselves are either actors or spectators, and of which we have a complete knowledge, nothing being concealed from us; and knowing the good together with many other things that are displeasing to us, we are forced to conclude that the present is inferior to the past, though in reality it may be much more worthy of glory and fame. I do not speak of matters pertaining to the arts, which shine by their intrinsic merits, which time can neither add to nor diminish; but I speak of such things as pertain to the actions and manners of men, of which we do not possess such manifest evidence.

I repeat, then, that this practice of praising and decrying is very general, though it cannot be said that it is always erroneous; for sometimes our judgement is of necessity correct, human affairs being in a state of perpetual movement, always either ascending or declining. We see, for instance, a city or country with a government well-organized by some man of superior ability; for a time it progresses and attains a great prosperity through the talents of its lawgiver. Now if anyone living at such a period should praise the past more than the time in which he lives, he would certainly be deceiving himself; and this error will be found due to the reasons above indicated. But should he live in that city or country at the period after it shall have passed the zenith of its glory and in the time of its decline, then he would not be wrong in praising the past. Reflecting now upon the course of human affairs, I think that, as a whole, the world remains very much in the same condition, and the good in it always balances the evil; but the good and evil change from one country to another, as we learn from the history of those ancient kingdoms that differed from each other in manners, while the world at large remained the same. . . .

But to return to our argument, I say that if men's judgment is at fault upon the point of whether the present age be better than the past, of which the latter, owing to its antiquity, they cannot have such perfect knowledge as of their own period, the judgment of old men of what they have seen in their youth and in their old age should not be false, inasmuch as they have equally seen both the one and the other. This would be true if men at the different periods of their lives had the same judgment and the same appetites. But as these vary (though the times do not), things cannot appear the same to men who have other tastes, other delights, and other considerations in age from what they had in youth. For as men when they age lose their strength and energy, while their prudence and judgment improve, so the same things that in youth appeared to them supportable and good, will of necessity, when they have grown old, seem to them insupportable and evil; and when they should blame their own judgment they find fault with the times. Moreover, as human desires are insatiable (because their nature is to have and to do everything while fortune limits their possessions and capacity of enjoyment), this gives rise to a constant discontent in the human mind and a weariness of the things they possess; and it is this which makes them decry the present, praise the past and desire the future, and all this without any reasonable motive. I know not, then, whether I deserve to be classed with those who deceive themselves, if in these Discourses I shall laud too much the times of ancient Rome and censure those of our own day. And truly, if the virtues that ruled then and the vices that prevail now were not as clear as the sun, I should be more reticent in my expressions, lest I should fall into the very error for which I reproach others. But the matter being so manifest that everybody sees it, I shall boldly and openly say what I think of the former times and of the present, so as to excite in the minds of the young men who may read my writings the desire to avoid the evils of the latter, and to prepare themselves to imitate the virtues of the former, whenever fortune presents them the occasion. For it is the duty of an honest man to teach others that good which the malignity of the times and of fortune has prevented his doing himself; so that amongst the many capable ones whom he has instructed, someone perhaps, more favored by Heaven, may perform it. (*D*, II:introduction)

[W]e will premise that all cities are founded either by natives of the country or by strangers. The little security which the natives found in living dispersed; the impossibility for each to resist isolated, either because of the situation or because of their small number, the attacks of any enemy that might present himself; the difficulty of uniting in time for defense at his approach, and the necessity of abandoning the greater number of their retreats, which quickly became a prize to the assailant -- such were the motives that caused the first inhabitants of a country to build cities for the purpose of escaping these dangers. They resolved, of their own accord, or by the advice of someone who had most authority amongst them, to live together in some place of their selection that might offer them greater conveniences and greater facility of defense. (*D*, I:1)

[S]ome of the [ancient] writers on politics distinguished three kinds of government, viz., the monarchical, the aristocratic, and the democratic; and maintain that the legislators of a people must choose from these three the one that seems to them most suitable. Other authors, wiser according to the opinion of many, count six kinds of government, three of which are very bad, and three good in themselves, but so liable to be corrupted that they become absolutely bad. The three good ones are those which we have just named; the three bad ones result from the degradation of the other three, and each of them resembles its corresponding original, so that the transition from the one to the other is very easy. Thus monarchy becomes tyranny; aristocracy degenerates into oligarchy; and popular government lapses readily into licentiousness. So that a legislator who gives to a state which he founds either of these three forms of government, constitutes it but for a brief time; for no precautions can prevent either one of the three that are reputed good from degenerating into its opposite kind; so great are in these the attractions and resemblances between the good and the evil.

Chance has given birth to these different kinds of governments amongst men; for at the beginning of the world the inhabitants were few in number, and lived for a time dispersed like beasts. As the human race increased, the necessity for uniting themselves for defense made itself felt; the better to attain this object, they chose the strongest and most courageous from amongst themselves and placed him at their head, promising to obey him. Thence they began to know the good and the honest, and to distinguish them from the bad and the vicious; for seeing a man injure his benefactors aroused at once two sentiments in every heart: hatred against the ingrate and love for the benefactor. They blamed the first, and on the contrary, honored those the more who showed themselves grateful, for each felt that he in turn might be subject to a like wrong; and to prevent similar evils, they set to work to make laws, and to institute punishments for those who contravened them. Such was the origin of justice. This caused them, when they had afterwards to choose a prince, neither to look to the strongest nor bravest, but to the wisest and most just. But when they began to make sovereignty hereditary and non-elective, the children quickly degenerated from their fathers; and so far from trying to equal their virtues, they considered that a prince had nothing else to do than to excel all the rest in luxury, indulgence, and every other variety of pleasure. The prince consequently soon drew upon himself the general hatred. An object of hatred, he naturally felt fear; fear in turn dictated to him precautions and wrongs, and thus tyranny quickly developed itself. Such were the beginning and causes of disorders, conspiracies, and plots against the sovereigns, set on foot not by the feeble and timid, but by those citizens who, surpassing the others in grandeur of soul, in wealth and in courage, could not submit to the outrages and excesses of their princes.

Under such powerful leaders the masses armed themselves against the tyrant, and after having rid themselves of him, submitted to these chiefs as their liberators. These, abhorring the very name of prince, constituted themselves a new government; and at first, bearing in mind the past tyranny, they governed in strict accordance with the laws which they had established themselves; preferring public interests to their own, and to administer and protect with greatest care both public and private affairs. The children succeeded their fathers, and ignorant of the changes of fortune, having never experienced its reverses, and indisposed to remain content with this civil equality, they in turn gave themselves up to cupidity, ambition, libertinage, and violence, and soon caused the aristocratic government to degenerate into an oligarchic tyranny, regardless of all civil rights. They soon, however, experienced the same fate as the first tyrant; the people, disgusted with their government, placed themselves at the command of whoever was willing to attack them, and this disposition soon produced an avenger, who was sufficiently well-seconded to destroy them. The memory of the prince and the wrongs committed by him being still fresh in their minds, and having overthrown the oligarchy, the people were not willing to return to the government of a prince. A popular government was therefore resolved upon, and it was so organized that the authority should not again fall into the hands of a prince or a small number of nobles. And as all governments are first looked up to with some degree of reverence, the popular state also maintained itself for a time, but which was never of long duration, and lasted generally only about as long as the generation that had established it; for it soon ran into that kind of license which inflicts injury upon public as well as private interests. Each individual only consulted his own passions, and a thousand acts of injustice were daily committed, so that, constrained by necessity, or directed by the counsels of some good man, or for the purpose of escaping from this anarchy, they returned anew to the government of a prince, and from this they generally lapsed again into anarchy, step by step, in the same manner and from the same causes as we have indicated.

Such is the circle which all republics are destined to run through. Seldom, however, do they come back to the original form of government, which results from the fact that their duration is not sufficiently long to be able to undergo these repeated changes and preserve their existence. But it may well happen that a republic lacking strength and good council in its difficulties becomes subject after a while to some neighboring state that is better organized than itself; and if such is not the case, then they will be apt to revolve indefinitely in the circle of revolutions. I say, then, that all kinds of government are defective; those three which we have qualified as good because they are too short-lived, and the three bad ones because of their inherent viciousness. Thus sagacious legislators, knowing the vices of each of these systems of government by themselves, have chosen one that should partake of all of them, judging that to be the most stable and solid. In fact, when there is combined under the same constitution a prince, a nobility, and the power of the people, then these three powers will watch and keep each other reciprocally in cheek. (*D*, I:2)

All those who have written upon civil institutions demonstrate (and history is full of examples to support them) that whoever desires to found a state and give it laws, must start with assuming that all men are bad and ever ready to display their vicious nature whenever they may find occasion for it. If their evil disposition remains concealed for a time, it must be attributed to some unknown reason; and we must assume that it lacked occasion to show itself; but time, which has been said to be the father of all truth, does not fail to bring it to light. (*D*, I:3)

Of all men who have been eulogized, those deserve it most who have been the authors and founders of religions; next come such as have established republics or kingdoms. After these the most celebrated are those who have commanded armies, and have extended the possessions of their kingdom or country. To these may be added literary men, but as these are of different kinds, they are celebrated according to their respective degrees of excellence. All others -- and their number is infinite -- receive such share of praise as pertains to the exercise of their arts and professions. On the contrary, those are doomed to infamy and universal execration who have destroyed religions, who have overturned republics and kingdoms, who are enemies of virtue, of letters, and of every art that is useful and honorable to mankind. Such are the impious and violent, the ignorant and the idle, the vile and degraded. And there are none so foolish or so wise, so wicked or so good, that, in choosing between these two qualities, they do not praise what is praiseworthy and blame that which deserves blame. And yet nearly all men, deceived by a false good and a false glory, allow themselves voluntarily or ignorantly to be drawn towards those who deserve more blame than praise. Such as by the establishment of a republic or kingdom could earn eternal glory for themselves incline to tyranny, without perceiving how much glory, how much honor, security, satisfaction, and tranquillity of mind, they forfeit; and what infamy, disgrace, blame, danger, and disquietude they incur. And it is impossible that those who have lived as private citizens in a republic, or those who by fortune or courage have risen to be princes of the same, if they were to read history and take the records of antiquity for example, should not prefer Scipio to Caesar. (*D*, I:10)

Many examples in ancient history prove how difficult it is for a people that has been accustomed to live under the government of a prince to preserve its liberty, if by some accident it has recovered it, as was the case with Rome after the expulsion of the Tarquins. And this difficulty is a reasonable one; for such a people may well be compared to some wild animal, which (although by nature ferocious and savage) has been, as it were, subdued by having been always kept imprisoned and in servitude, and being let out into the open fields, not knowing how to provide food and shelter for itself, becomes an easy prey to the first one who attempts to chain it up again. The same thing happens to a people that has not been accustomed to self-government; for, ignorant of all public affairs, of all means of defense or offense, neither knowing the princes nor being known by them, it soon relapses under a yoke, oftentimes much heavier than the one which it had but just shaken off. This difficulty occurs even when the body of the people is not wholly corrupt; but when corruption has taken possession of the whole people, then it cannot preserve its free condition even for the shortest possible time . . .; and therefore our argument has reference to a people where corruption has not yet become general, and where the good still prevails over the bad. To the above comes another difficulty, which is that the state that becomes free makes enemies for itself and not friends. All those become its enemy who were benefited by the tyrannical abuses and fattened upon the treasures of the prince, and who being now deprived of these advantages cannot remain content, and are therefore driven to attempt to reestablish the tyranny so as to recover their former authority and advantages. A state then, as I have said, that becomes free, makes no friends; for free government bestows honors and rewards only according to certain honest and fixed rules, outside of which there are neither the one nor the other. And such as obtain these honors and rewards do not consider themselves under obligations to anyone because they believe that they were entitled to them by their merits. Besides the advantages that result to the mass of the people from a free government, such as to be able freely to enjoy one's own without apprehension, to have nothing to fear for the honor of his wife and daughters, or for himself -- all these, I say, are not appreciated by anyone while he is in the enjoyment of them; for no one will confess himself under obligation to anyone merely because he has not been injured by him.

Thus it is that a state that has freshly achieved liberty makes enemies and no friends. And to prevent this inconvenience, and the disorders which are apt to come with it, there is no remedy more powerful, valid, healthful, and necessary than the killing of the sons of Brutus . . . (*D*, I:16)

Whoever considers the past and the present will readily observe that all cities and all peoples are and ever have been animated by the same desires and the same passions; so that it is easy, by diligent study of the past, to foresee what is likely to happen in the future in any republic, and to apply those remedies that were used by the ancients, or not finding any that were employed by them, to devise new ones from the similarity of the events. But as such considerations are neglected or not understood by most of those who read, or if understood by these are unknown by those who govern, it follows that the same troubles generally recur in all republics. (*D*, I:39)

And certainly a country can never be united and happy, except when it obeys wholly one government, whether a republic or a monarchy . . . (*D*, I:12)

[O]nly those cities and countries that are free can achieve greatness. Population is greater there because marriages are more free and offer more advantages to the citizen; for people will gladly have children when they know that they can support them, and that they will not be deprived of their patrimony, and where they know that their children not only are born free and not slaves, but if they possess talents and virtue, can arrive at the highest dignities of the state. In free countries we also see wealth increase more rapidly, both that which results from the culture of the soil and that which is produced by industry and art; for everybody gladly multiplies those things, and seeks to acquire those goods the possession of which he can tranquilly enjoy. Thence men vie with each other to increase both private and public wealth, which consequently increase in an extraordinary manner. But the contrary of all this takes place in countries that are subject to another; and the more rigorous the subjugation of the people, the more will they be deprived of all the good to which they had previously been accustomed. (*D*, II:2)

For where the very safety of the country depends upon the resolution to be taken, no considerations of justice or injustice, humanity or cruelty, nor of glory or of shame, should be allowed to prevail. But putting all other considerations aside, the only question should be, what course will save the life and liberty of the country? (*D*, III:41)

As to those who prefer a government more inclusive than [a quasi-principality], I say that unless it is inclusive in such a way that it will become a well-ordered republic, its inclusiveness is likely to make it fall more rapidly. And if they will explicitly tell how they would like it organized, I shall give an explicit answer, but since they continue in generalities, I am not able to answer other than generally. I believe the following answer alone is enough; . . . No firm government can be devised if it is not either a true princedom or a true republic, because all the constitutions between these two are defective. The reason is entirely evident, because the princedom has just one path to dissolution, that is, to descend toward the republic. And similarly the republic has just one path toward being dissolved, that is, to rise toward a princedom. Governments of a middle sort have two ways: they can rise toward the princedom and descend toward the republic. From this comes their lack of firmness. (*GF*)

[I]n all cities where the citizens are accustomed to equality, a princedom cannot be set up except with the utmost difficulty, and in those cities where the citizens are accustomed to inequality, a republic cannot be set up except with the utmost difficulty. In order to form a republic in Milan, where inequality among the citizens is great, necessarily all the nobility must be destroyed and brought to an equality with the others, because among them are men so above all rules that the laws are not enough to hold them down, but there must be a living voice and a kingly power to hold them down. On the contrary, in order to have a princedom in Florence, where equality is great, the establishment of inequality would be necessary; noble lords of walled towns and boroughs would have to be set up, who in support of the prince would with their arms and their followers stifle the city and the whole province. A prince alone, lacking a nobility, cannot support the weight of a princedom; for that reason it is necessary that between him and the generality of the people there should be a middle group that will help him support it. This can be seen in all the states with a prince, and especially in the kingdom of France, where the gentlemen rule the people, the princes the gentlemen, and the king the princes. (*GF*)

Without satisfying the generality of citizens, to set up a stable government is impossible. (*GF*)

All the cities that ever at any time have been ruled by an absolute prince, by aristocrats or by the people, as is [Florence], have had for their protection force combined with prudence, because the latter is not enough alone, and the first either does not produce things or when they are produced, does not maintain them. Force and prudence, then, are the might of all governments that ever have been or will be in the world. Hence any man who has considered change of kingdoms and the destruction of provinces and of cities has not seen them caused by anything other than failure in arms or in good sense. (*AM*)

But if we consider the institutions of the ancients, we shall find that there is a very close, intimate relation between these two conditions [the civility of the citizen and the fierceness of the soldier], and that they are not only compatible and consistent with each other, but necessarily connected and interrelated. For all the arts that have been introduced into society for the common benefit of mankind, and all the ordinances that have been established to make them live in fear of God and in obedience to human laws, would be in vain and insignificant if they were not supported and defended by a military force; this force, when properly led and applied, will maintain those ordinances and keep up their authority, although they perhaps may not be perfect or flawless. But the best ordinances in the world will be despised and trampled under foot when they are not supported, as they ought to be, by a military power. (*AW*, preface)

But to give a rule which may be observed by any state, I say that every prince or republic should select his men [for military service] from his own dominions, whether hot, cold, or temperate; for we see by ancient examples that good discipline and exercise will make good soldiers in any country, and that the defects of nature may be supplied by art and industry -- which in this case is more effective than nature itself. (*AW*, I)

[F]or inexperience is the mother of cowardice, and compulsion makes men mutinous and discontented; but both experience and courage are acquired by arming, exercising, and disciplining men properly . . . As to the matter of compulsion, I reply that men selected by their prince's command should be neither all volunteers nor forcibly compelled into the service, for if they were all volunteers, the mischiefs which I just now mentioned would ensue, it could not properly be called a *delectus* [selection], and few would be willing to serve. Compulsion, on the other hand, would be accompanied by no fewer inconveniences; therefore, a middle course ought to be taken whereby -- without either using men with outright violence or depending entirely upon their own voluntary offers -- they may be motivated by the obedience they think due to their governors to expose themselves to a little immediate hardship, rather than incur their displeasure; and by these means (since their own will seems to cooperate with a gentle sort of compulsion) you will easily prevent those evils that might otherwise result from a spirit of licentiousness or discontent. (*AW*, I)

I shall convince you how little foundation there is for your objection that such a citizens' militia, under the command of an aspiring subject or citizen, may deprive a prince or republic of his authority and dominions; for it is certain that no subjects or citizens, when legally armed and kept in due order by their masters, ever did the least mischief to any state. On the contrary, they have always been of the highest service to all governments and have kept them free and incorrupt longer than they would have been without them. Rome remained free for four hundred years and Sparta eight hundred, although their citizens were armed all that time; but many other states that have been disarmed have lost their liberties in less than forty years. No state, therefore, can support itself without an army. If a state has no soldiers of its own, it must be forced to hire foreign troops; this will be much more dangerous because they are more likely to be corrupted and become subservient to the ambition of a powerful citizen who -- when he has nobody to deal with but an unarmed and defenseless multitude -- may easily avail himself of its assistance to overturn the established government. Besides, every state must naturally be more afraid of two enemies than of one; and the one taking foreign troops into its pay must be apprehensive of them, as well as of its own forces. (*AW*, I)

I shall only lay it down as a certain truth, that no man has ever founded a monarchy or a republic without being well-assured that if his subjects were armed, they would always be ready and willing to defend the monarchy or republic. (*AW*, I)

[T]yranny and usurpation are not a result of arming the citizens, but of leading a government weakly, and that while a state is well led it has nothing to fear from its subjects' arms. (*AW*, I)

Those who talk of raising a militia, therefore, and of paying them when they have nothing for them to do, talk of things that either are impossible or will serve no purpose; but it is highly necessary, I admit, to pay them -- and well too -- when they are called out to serve their country. However, if such a regulation should happen to cause the community some inconvenience during peacetime -- which can hardly be -- surely that must be greatly counter-balanced by the conveniences and advantages resulting from it, for without a regular and well-ordered militia people cannot live in security. (*AW*, I)

[A] state ought to depend upon only those troops composed of its own subjects; that those subjects cannot be better raised than by a citizens' militia; and that there can be no better method devised to form an army or to introduce good order and discipline among soldiers. (*AW*, I)

Now men become excellent and show their *virtù* according to how they are employed and encouraged by their sovereigns, whether these happen to be kings, princes, or heads of republics. (*AW*, II)

[T]he love of money ordinarily operates as strongly upon men as love of their life. (*AW*, IV)

II. Law and the Legislator

It is a great good fortune for a republic to have a legislator sufficiently wise to give her laws so regulated that, without the necessity of correcting them, they afford security to those who live under them. (*D*, I:2)

All the legislators that have given wise constitutions to republics have deemed it an essential precaution to establish a guard and protection to liberty; and according as this was more or less wisely placed, liberty endured a greater or less length of time (*D*, I:5)

If anyone . . . wishes to establish an entirely new republic, he will have to consider whether he wishes to have her expand in power and dominion like Rome, or whether he intends to confine her within narrow limits. In the first case, it will be necessary to organize her as Rome was, and submit to dissensions and troubles as best he may; for without a great number of men, and these well-armed, no republic can ever increase. In the second case, he may organize her like Sparta and Venice; but as expansion is the poison of such republics, he must by every means in his power prevent her from making conquests, for such acquisitions by a feeble republic always prove their ruin . . . (*D*, I:6)

I think, then, that to found a republic which should endure a long time it would be best to organize her internally like Sparta, or to locate her, like Venice, in some strong place; and to make her sufficiently powerful, so that no one could hope to overcome her readily, and yet, on the other hand, not so powerful as to make her formidable to her neighbors. In this way she might long enjoy her independence. For there are but two motives for making war against a republic: one, the desire to subjugate her; the other, the apprehension of being subjugated by her. The two means which we have indicated remove, as it were, both these pretexts for war; for if the republic is difficult to be conquered, her defenses being well-organized, as I presuppose, then it will seldom or never happen that anyone will venture upon the project of conquering her. If she remains quite within her limits, and experience shows that she entertains no ambitious projects, the fear of her power will never prompt anyone to attack her; and this would even be more certainly the case if her constitution and laws prohibited all aggrandizement. And I certainly think that if she could be kept in this equilibrium it would be the best political existence, and would insure to any state real tranquillity. But as all human things are kept in a perpetual movement, and can never remain stable, states naturally either rise or decline, and necessity compels them to many acts to which reason will not influence them; so that having organized a republic competent to maintain herself without expanding, still, if forced by necessity to extend her territory, in such case we shall see her foundations give way and herself quickly brought to ruin. And thus, on the other hand, if Heaven favors her so as never to be involved in war, the continued tranquillity would enervate her, or provoke internal dissensions, which together, or either of them separately, will be apt to prove her ruin. Seeing then the impossibility of establishing in this respect a perfect equilibrium, and that a precise middle course cannot be maintained, it is proper in the organization of a republic to select the most honorable course, and to constitute her so that, even if necessity should oblige her to expand, she may yet be able to preserve her acquisitions. . . . I believe it therefore necessary rather to take the constitution of Rome as a model than that of any other republic (for I do not believe that a middle course between the two can be found) and to tolerate the differences that will arise between the Senate and the people as an unavoidable inconvenience in achieving greatness like that of Rome. (*D*, I:6)

No more useful and necessary authority can be given to those who are appointed as guardians of the liberty of a state, than the faculty of accusing the citizens to the people, or to any magistrate or council, for any attempt against public liberty. Such a system has two very marked advantages for a republic. This first is that the apprehension of being accused prevents the citizens from attempting anything against the state, and should they nevertheless attempt it, they are immediately punished without regard to person. The other is that it affords a way for those evil dispositions that arise in one way or another against some one citizen to vent themselves; and when these ferments cannot in some way exhaust themselves, their promoters are apt to resort to some extraordinary means that may lead to the ruin of the republic. Nothing, on the other hand, renders a republic more firm and stable than to organize it in such a way that the excitement of the ill humors that agitate a state may have a way prescribed by law for venting itself. (*D*, I:7)

[The experience of Rome] shows . . . how useful and necessary it is for a republic to have laws that afford to the masses the opportunity of giving vent to the hatred they may have conceived against any citizen; for if there exist no legal means for this, they will resort to illegal ones, which beyond doubt produce much worse effects. For ordinarily when a citizen is oppressed, and even if an injustice is committed against him, it rarely causes any disturbance in the republic; for this oppression has been effected by neither private nor foreign forces, which are most destructive to public liberty, but is effected solely by the public force of the state in accordance with the established laws, which have their prescribed limits that cannot be transcended to the injury of the republic. (*D*, I:7)

[Roman history shows] how much detested calumnies are in republics, as well as under any other government, and that no means should be left unemployed to repress them in time. Now, there is no more effectual way for putting an end to calumnies than to introduce the system of legal accusations, which will be as beneficial to republics as calumnies are injurious. On the other hand, there is this difference, namely, that calumnies require neither witnesses, nor confrontings, nor any particulars to prove them, so that every citizen may be calumniated by another, while accusations cannot be lodged against anyone without being accompanied by positive proofs and circumstances that demonstrate the truth of the accusation. Accusations must be brought before the magistrates, or the people, or the councils, while calumnies are spread in public places as well as in private dwellings; and calumnies are more practiced where the system of accusations does not exist, and in cities the constitution of which does not admit of them. The lawgiver of a republic, therefore, should give every citizen the right to accuse another citizen without fear or suspicion; and this being done, and properly carried out, he should severely punish calumniators, who would have no right to complain of such punishment, it being open to them to bring charges against those whom they had in private calumniated. And where this system is not well-established there will always be great disorders, for calumnies irritate, but do not chastise men; and those who have been thus irritated will think of strengthening themselves, hating more than fearing the slanders spread against them. (*D*, I:8)

[A]s a general rule . . . it never or rarely happens that a republic or monarchy is well-constituted, or its old institutions entirely reformed, unless it is done by only one individual; it is even necessary that he whose mind has conceived such a constitution should be alone in carrying it into effect. A sagacious legislator of a republic, therefore, whose object is to promote the public good, and not his private interests, and who prefers his country to his own successors, should concentrate all authority in himself; and a wise mind will never censure anyone for having employed any extraordinary means for the purpose of establishing a kingdom or constituting a republic. It is well that, when the act accuses him, the result should excuse him; and when the result is good . . . it will always absolve him from blame. For he is to be reprehended who commits violence for the purpose of destroying, and not he who employs it for beneficent purposes. The lawgiver should, however, be sufficiently wise and virtuous not to leave this authority which he has assumed either to his heirs or to anyone else; for mankind, being more prone to evil than to good, his successor might employ for evil purposes the power which he had used only for good ends. Besides, although one man alone should organize a government, yet it will not endure long enough if the administration of it remains on the shoulders of a single individual; it is well, then, to confide this to the charge of many, for thus it will be sustained by the many. Therefore, as the organization of anything cannot be made by many, because the divergence of their opinions hinders them from agreeing as to what is best, yet when once they do not understand it, they will not readily agree to abandon it. . . . Considering, then, all these things, I conclude that, to found a republic, one must be alone. (*D*, I:9)

And thus it is seen in all human affairs, upon careful examination, that you cannot avoid one inconvenience without incurring another. If therefore you wish to make a people numerous and warlike, so as to create a great empire, you will have to constitute it in such manner as will cause you more difficulty in managing it; and if you keep it either small or unarmed, and you acquire other dominions, you will not be able to hold them, or you will become so feeble that you will fall a prey to whoever attacks you. And therefore in all our decisions we must consider well what presents the least inconveniences, and then choose the best, for we shall never find any course entirely free from objections. (*D*, I:6)

[M]en act rightly only upon compulsion; but from the moment that they have the option and liberty to commit wrong with impunity, then they never fail to carry confusion and disorder everywhere. It is this that has caused it to be said that poverty and hunger make men industrious, and that the law makes men good; and if fortunate circumstances cause good to be done without constraint, the law may be dispensed with. But when such happy influence is lacking, then the law immediately becomes necessary. (*D*, I:3)

[W]hen any evil arises within a republic or threatens it from without, that is to say, from an intrinsic or extrinsic cause, and has become so great as to fill everyone with apprehension, the more certain remedy by far is to temporize with it, rather than to attempt to extirpate it; for almost invariably he who attempts to crush it will rather increase its force, and will accelerate the harm apprehended from it. And such evils arise more frequently in republics from intrinsic than extrinsic causes, as it often occurs that a citizen is allowed to acquire more authority than is proper; or that changes are permitted in a law which is the very nerve and life of liberty; and then they let this evil go so far that it becomes more hazardous to correct it than to allow it to run on. And it is the more difficult to recognize these evils at their origin, as it seems natural to men always to favor the beginning of things; and these favors are more readily accorded to such acts as seem to have some merit in them, and are done by young men. For if in a republic a noble youth is seen to rise, who is possessed of some extraordinary merits, the eyes of all citizens quickly turn to him, and all hasten to show him honor, regardless of consequences; so that, if he is in anyway ambitious, the gifts of nature and the favor of his fellow citizens will soon raise him to such a height that, when the citizens become sensible of the error they have committed, they have no longer the requisite means for checking him, and their efforts to employ such as they have will only accelerate his advance to power . . .

I say, then, that inasmuch as it is difficult to know these evils at their first origin, owing to an illusion which all new things are apt to produce, the wiser course is to temporize with such evils when they are recognized, instead of violently attacking them; for by temporizing with them they will either die out of themselves, or at least their worst results will be long deferred. And princes or magistrates who wish to destroy such evils must watch all points, and must be careful in attacking them not to increase instead of diminishing them, for they must not believe that a fire can be extinguished by blowing upon it. They should carefully examine the extent and force of the evil, and if they think themselves sufficiently strong to combat it, then they should attack it regardless of consequences; otherwise they should let it be, and in no wise attempt it. (*D*, I:33)

[T]he customary proceedings of republics are slow, no magistrate or council being permitted to act independently, but being in almost all instances obliged to act in concert one with the other, so that often much time is required to harmonize their several opinions; and tardy measures are most dangerous when the occasion requires prompt action. And therefore all republics should have some institution similar to dictatorship. . . . And when a republic lacks some such system, a strict observance of the established laws will expose her to ruin; or to save her from such danger the laws will have to be disregarded. Now in a well-ordered republic it should never be necessary to resort to extra-constitutional measures; for although they may for the time be beneficial, yet the precedent is pernicious, for if the practice is once established of disregarding the laws for good objects, they will in a little while be disregarded under that pretext for evil purposes. Thus no republic will ever be perfect if she has not by law provided for everything, having a remedy for every emergency, and fixed rules for applying it. And therefore I will say, in conclusion, that those republics which in time of danger cannot resort to a dictatorship, or some similar authority, will generally be ruined when grave occasions occur. (*D*, I:34)

[T]o attempt to eradicate an abuse that has grown up in a republic by the enactment of retrospective laws is a most inconsiderate proceeding, and . . . only serves to accelerate the fatal results which the abuse tends to bring about; but by temporizing, the end will either be delayed, or the evil will exhaust itself before it attains that end. (*D*, I:37)

[Y]et it [is] inconsistent with a proper regard for liberty to violate the law, and especially one . . . recently made. For I think that there can be no worse example in a republic than to make a law and not to observe it; the more so when it is disregarded by the very parties who made it. (*D*, I:45)

[I]t is not well that a republic should be constituted in such fashion that a citizen can be oppressed without recourse for having promulgated a law for the benefit of liberty. (*D*, I:49)

[O]ne of the most important points to be considered by him who wishes to establish a republic is the question, in whose hands he shall place the power over the life and death of its citizens. The constitution of Rome was excellent upon this point, for there an appeal to the people was the ordinary practice, and when an important case occurred, where it would have been perilous to delay execution by such an appeal, they had recourse to the Dictator, who had the right of immediate execution; this, however, was resorted to only in cases of extreme necessity. But in Florence, and in other cities who like her had their origin in servitude, the power of life and death was lodged in the hands of a stranger, sent by the prince to exercise that power. When these cities afterwards became free, they left that power in the hands of a foreigner, whom they called "the Captain." But the facility with which he could be corrupted by the powerful citizens made this a most pernicious system; and in the course of the mutations of their governments that system was changed, and a council of eight citizens was appointed to perform the functions of the Captain; which only made matters worse, for the reason . . . that a tribunal of a few is always under the control of a few powerful citizens. (*D*, I:49)

I say, then, that individual men, and especially princes, may be charged with the same defects of which writers accuse the people; for whoever is not controlled by laws will commit the same errors as an unbridled multitude. This may easily be verified, for there have been and still are plenty of princes, and a few good and wise ones, such, I mean, as needed not the curb that controlled them. (*D*, I:58)

[I]t is impossible to explain one's self properly when in doubt and indecision as to what is to be done; but once resolved and decided, it is easy to find suitable words. I have the more willingly remarked upon this point as I have often known such indecision to interfere with proper public action, to the detriment and shame of our republic. And it will always happen that in doubtful cases, where prompt resolution is required, there will be this indecision when weak men have to deliberate and resolve. Slow and dilatory deliberations are not less injurious than indecision, especially when you have to decide in favor of an ally; for tardiness helps no one, and generally injures yourself. It ordinarily arises from lack of courage or force, or from the evil disposition of those who have to deliberate, being influenced by passion to ruin the state or to serve some personal interests, and who therefore do not allow the deliberations to proceed, but thwart and impede them in every way. Good citizens, therefore, never impede deliberations, especially in matters that admit of no delay, even if they see the popular impulse tending to a dangerous course. (*D*, II:15)

Those who have been present at any deliberative assemblies of men will have observed how erroneous their opinions often are; and in fact, unless they are directed by superior men, they are apt to be contrary to all reason. But as superior men in corrupt republics (especially in periods of peace and quiet) are generally hated, either from jealousy or the ambition of others, it follows that the preference is given to what common error approves, or to what is suggested by men who are more desirous of pleasing the masses than of promoting the general good. When, however, adversity comes, then the error is discovered, and then the people fly to safety to those whom in prosperity they had neglected . . . Certain events also easily misled men who have not a great deal of experience, for they have in them so much that resembles truth that men easily persuade themselves that they are correct in the judgment they have formed upon the subject. (*D*, II:22)

But all these diversities of opinions and modes of governing spring from the weakness of those who are at the head of governments, and who, lacking the requisite force and energy to preserve their states, resort to such expedients [as nurturing faction]; which in times of tranquillity may occasionally be of service, but when trouble and adversity come, then their fallacy becomes manifest. (*D*, III:27)

I believe the greatest honor possible for men to have is that willingly given them by their native cities; I believe the greatest good to be done and the most pleasing to God is that which one does to one's native city. Besides this, no man is so much exalted by any act of his as are those men who have with laws and with institutions remodeled republics and kingdoms; these are, after those who have been gods, the first to be praised. And because they have been few who have had the opportunity to do it, and very few those who have understood how to do it, small is the number who have done it. And so much has this glory been esteemed by men seeking for nothing other than glory that when unable to form a republic in reality, they have done it in writing, as Aristotle, Plato, and many others, who have wished to show the world that if they have not founded a free government, as did Solon and Lycurgus, they have failed not through their ignorance, but through their impotence for putting it into practice. (*GF*)

Those who organize a republic ought to provide for the three different sorts of men who exist in all cities, namely, the most important, those in the middle, and the lowest. And though in Florence the citizens possess the equality mentioned above, nonetheless some of her citizens have ambitious spirits and think they deserve to outrank the others; these must be satisfied in organizing a republic; the last government [the Republic of 1494-1512], indeed, fell for no other cause than that such a group was not satisfied. To men of this sort it is not possible to give satisfaction unless dignity is given to the highest offices in the republic, which dignity is to be maintained in their persons. (*GF*)

III. Republics and Republicanism

[E]very free state ought to afford the people the opportunity of giving vent, so to say, to their ambition; and above all those republics which on important occasions have to avail themselves of this very people. (*D*, I:4)

But just as useful as accusations are in a republic, just so useless and pernicious are calumnies . . . (*D*, I:7)

For if . . . two successive good and valorous princes are sufficient to conquer the world, as was the case with Philip of Macedon and Alexander the Great, a republic should be able to do still more, having the power to elect not only two successions, but an infinite number of most competent and virtuous rulers one after the other; and this system of electing a succession of virtuous men should ever be the established practice of every republic. (*D*, I:20)

In reading the history of republics we find in all of them a degree of ingratutude to their citizens. (*D*, I:28)

[N]o well-ordered republic should ever cancel the crimes of its citizens by their merits; but having established rewards for good actions and penalties for evil ones, and having rewarded a citizen for good conduct who afterwards commits a wrong, he should be chastised for that without regard to his previous merits. And a state that properly observes this principle will long enjoy its liberty; but if otherwise, it will speedily come to ruin. For if a citizen who has rendered some eminent service to the state should add to the reputation and influence which he has thereby acquired the confident audacity of being able to commit any wrong without fear of punishment, he will in a little while become so insolent and overbearing as to put an end to all power of the law. But to preserve a wholesome fear of punishment for evil deeds, it is necessary not to omit rewarding good ones as has been seen was done by Rome. And although a republic may be poor and able to give but little, yet she should not abstain from giving that little; for even the smallest reward for good action -- no matter how important the service to the state -- will always be esteemed by the recipient as most honorable. (*D*, I:24)

[The faults] resulting from the desire to preserve liberty are, amongst others, the following: namely, to injure those citizens whom she should reward, and to suspect those in whom she should place the most confidence. And although the effects of such conduct occasion great evils in a republic that is already corrupt, and which often lead to despotism . . . still, in a republic not yet entirely corrupt, they may be productive of great good in preserving her freedom for a greater length of time, as the dread of punishment will keep men better and less ambitious. (*D*, I:29)

[I]t is the magistracies and powers that are created by illegitimate means which harm a republic, and not those that are appointed in the regular way. (*D*, I:34)

[B]efore a citizen can be in a position to usurp extraordinary powers, many things must concur, which in a republic as yet uncorrupted never can happen; for he must be exceedingly rich, and must have many adherents and partisans, which cannot be where the laws are observed; and even if he had them he would never be supported by the free suffrages of the people, for such men are generally looked upon as dangerous. (*D*, I:34)

[T]he authority which is violently usurped, and not that which is conferred by the free suffrages of the people, is hurtful to republics. In this, however, there are two things to be considered; namely, the manner in which the authority is bestowed, and the length of time for which it is given. For when full power is conferred for any length of time (and I call a year or more a long time) it is always dangerous, and will be productive of good or ill effects, according as those upon whom it is conferred are themselves good or bad. . . . And therefore, when we said that an authority conferred by the free suffrages of the people never harmed a republic, we presupposed that the people, in giving that power, would limit it, as well as the time during which it was to be exercised. But if from having been deceived, or from any other reason, they are induced to give this power imprudently and in the way in which the Roman people gave it to the Decemvirs, then the same thing will happen to them as happened to the Romans. (*D*, I:35)

[I]t is the worst fault of feeble republics to be irresolute, so that whatever part they take is dictated by force; and if any good results from it, it is caused less by their sagacity than by their necessity. (*D*, I:38)

A republic can and should have more hope and confidence in that citizen who from a superior grade descends to accept a less important one, than in him who from an inferior employment mounts to the exercise of a superior one; for the latter cannot reasonably be relied upon unless he is surrounded by men of such respectability and virtue that his inexperience may in some measure be compensated for by their counsel and authority. (*D*, I:36)

[I]rresolute republics never take a wise course except by force; for their weakness never allows them to resolve upon anything where there is a doubt; and if that doubt is not overcome by some force, they remain forever in a state of suspense. (*D*, I:38)

[A]nd although we have maintained, in speaking of the Dictator, that only self-constituted authorities, and never those created by the people, are dangerous to liberty, yet when the people do create a magistracy, they should do it in such a way that magistrates should have some hesitation before they abuse their powers. (*D*, I:40)

The ambitious citizens of a republic seek in the first instance . . . to make themselves sure against the attacks, not only of individuals, but even of the magistrates. To enable them to do this they seek to gain friends, either by apparently honest ways, or by assisting men with money, or by defending them against the powerful; and as this seems virtuous, almost everybody is readily deceived by it, and therefore no one opposes it until the ambitious individual has, without hindrance, grown so powerful that private citizens fear him and the magistrates treat him with consideration. And when he has risen to that point, no one at the beginning having interfered with his greatness, it becomes in the end most dangerous to attempt to put him down, for the reasons I have given above when speaking of the danger of trying to abate an evil that has already attained a considerable growth in a city; so that in the end the matter is reduced to this, that you must endeavor to destroy the evil at the risk of sudden ruin, or by allowing it to go on, submit to manifest servitude, unless the death of the individual or some other accident intervenes to rid the state of him. For when it has once come to that point that the citizens and the magistrates are afraid to offend him and his adherents, it will afterwards not require much effort on his part to make them render judgments and attack persons according to his will. For this reason republics should make it one of their aims to watch that none of their citizens should be allowed to do harm on pretense of doing good, and that no one should acquire an influence that would injure instead of promote liberty. (*D*, I:46)

[T]he institutions of a city never should place it in the power of a few to interrupt all the important business of the republic. For instance, if you give to a council authority to distribute honors and offices, or devolve upon any magistracy the administration of a certain business, it is proper to impose upon them either the necessity of doing it under all circumstances, or to provide that, in case of their not doing it themselves, it can and shall be done by someone else; otherwise, the constitution would be defective upon this point, and likely to involve the state in great dangers, as we have seen would have been the case in Rome, if they could not have opposed the authority of the Tribunes to the obstinacy of the Consuls. (*D*, I:50)

For in truth there is no better nor easier mode in republics, and especially in such as are corrupt, for successfully opposing the ambition of any citizen, than to occupy in advance of him those ways by which he expects to attain the rank he aims at. (*D*, I:52)

[T]o explain more clearly what is meant by the term "gentlemen," I say that those are called gentlemen who live idly upon the proceeds of their extensive possessions, without devoting themselves to agriculture or any other useful pursuit to gain a living. Such men are pernicious to any country or republic; but more pernicious even than these are such as have, besides their other possessions, castles which they command, and subjects who obey them. . . . [F]or that class of men are everywhere enemies of all civil government. And to attempt the establishment of a republic in a country so constituted would be impossible. The only way to establish any kind of order there is to found a monarchical government; for where the body of the people is so thoroughly corrupt that the laws are powerless for restraint, it becomes necessary to establish some superior power which, with a royal hand, and with full and absolute powers, may put a curb upon the excessive ambition and corruption of the powerful. . . .

We may then draw the following conclusion from what has been said: that if anyone should wish to establish a republic in a country where there are many gentlemen, he will not succeed until he has destroyed them all; and whoever desires to establish a kingdom or principality where liberty and equality prevail, will equally fail, unless he withdraws from that general equality a number of the boldest and most ambitious spirits, and makes gentlemen of them, not merely in name but in fact, by giving to them castles and possessions, as well as money and subjects; so that surrounded by these he may be able to maintain his power, and that by his support they may satisfy their ambition, and the others may be constrained to submit to that yoke to which force alone has been able to subject them.

And as in this way definite relations will be established between the ruler and his subjects, each will be maintained in their respective ranks. But to establish a republic in a country better adapted to a monarchy, or a monarchy where a republic would be more suitable, requires a man of rare genius and power, and therefore out of the many that have attempted it but few have succeeded; for the greatness of the enterprise frightens men so that they fail even in the very beginning. Perhaps the opinion which I have expressed, that a republic cannot be established where there are gentlemen, may seem to be contradicted by the experience of the Venetian Republic, in which none but gentlemen could attain to any rank or public employment. And yet this example is in no way opposed to my theory, for the gentlemen of Venice are so more in name than in fact; for they have no great revenues from estates, their riches being founded upon commerce and movable property, and moreover none of them have castles or jurisdiction over subjects, but the name of gentlemen is only a title of dignity and respect, and is in no way based upon the things that gentlemen enjoy in other countries. And as all other republics have different classes under different names, so Venice is divided into gentlemen and commonalty, and the former have all the offices and honors, from which the latter are entirely excluded; and this distribution causes no disorders in that republic . . . Let republics, then, be established where equality exists, and, on the contrary, principalities where great inequality prevails; otherwise the governments will lack proper proportions and have but little durability. (*D*, I:55)

We see from the course of history that the Roman Republic, after the plebeians became entitled to the consulate, admitted all its citizens to this dignity without distinction of age or birth. In truth, age never formed a necessary qualification for public office; merit was the only consideration, whether found in young or old men. . . . Upon this subject much may be said. As regards birth, that point was conceded from necessity, and the same necessity that existed in Rome will be felt in every republic that aims to achieve the same success as Rome; for men cannot be made to bear labor and privations without the inducement of a corresponding reward, nor can they be deprived of such hope of reward without danger. . . . The state that does not admit its people to a share of its glory may treat them in its own way, as we have discussed elsewhere; but a state that wishes to undertake what Rome has done cannot make such a distinction.

And admitting that this may be so with regard to birth, then the question of age is necessarily also disposed of; for in electing a young man to an office which demands the prudence of an old man, it is necessary, if the election rests with the people, that he should have made himself worthy of that distinction by some extraordinary action. And when a young man has so much merit as to have distinguished himself by some notable action, it would be a great loss for this state not to be able to avail of his talents and services; and that he should have to wait until old age has robbed him of that vigor of mind and activity of which the state might have the benefit in his earlier age. (*D*, I:60)

[I]t is not individual prosperity, but the general good, that makes cities great; and certainly the general good is regarded nowhere but in republics, because whatever they do is for the common benefit, and should it happen to prove an injury to one or more individuals, those for whose benefit the thing is done are so numerous that they can always carry the measure against the few that are injured by it. But the very reverse happens where there is a prince whose private interests are generally in opposition to those of the city, while the measures taken for the benefit of the city are seldom deemed personally advantageous by the prince. This state of things soon leads to a tyranny, the least evil of which is to check the advance of the city in its career of prosperity, so that it grows neither in power nor wealth, but on the contrary rather retrogrades. And if fate should have it that the tyrant is enterprising, and by his courage and valor extends his dominions, it will never be for the benefit of the city, but only for his own; for he will never bestow honors and office upon the good and brave citizens over whom he tyrannizes, so that he may not have occasion to suspect and fear them. Nor will he make the states which he conquers subject or tributary to the city of which he is the despot, because it would not be to his advantage to make that city powerful, but it will always be for his interest to keep the state disunited, so that each place and country shall recognize him only as master; thus he alone and not his country profits by his conquests . . . It is no wonder, then, that the ancients hated tyranny and loved freedom, and that the very name of liberty should have been held in such high esteem by them . . . (*D*, II:2)

[A]n evil-disposed citizen cannot effect any changes for the worse in a republic, unless it be already corrupt. (*D*, III:8)

Conspiracies against the state are less dangerous for those engaged in them than plots against the life of the sovereign. In their conduct there is not so much danger, in their execution there is the same, and after execution there is none. In the conduct of the plot the danger is very slight, for a citizen may aspire to supreme power without manifesting his intentions to anyone; and if nothing interferes with his plans, he may carry them through successfully, or if they are thwarted by some law, he may await a more favorable moment, and attempt it by another way. This is understood to apply to a republic that is already partially corrupted; for in one not yet tainted by corruption such thoughts could never enter the mind of any citizen. Citizens of a republic, then, may by a variety of ways and means aspire to sovereign authority without incurring great risks. If republics are slower than princes, they are also less suspicious, and therefore less cautious; and if they show more respect to their great citizens, these in turn are thereby made more daring and audacious in conspiring against them. (*D*, III:6)

A republic should take great care not to entrust with an important administration one who has been gravely offended. (*D*, III:17)

I believe that in such cases which involve imminent peril there will be found somewhat more of stability in republics than in princes. For even if the republics were inspired by the same feelings and intentions as the princes, yet the fact of their movements being slower will make them take more time in forming resolutions, and therefore they will less promptly break their faith.

Alliances are broken from considerations of interest; and in this respect republics are much more careful in the observance of treaties than princes. It would be easy to cite instances where the princes for the smallest advantage have broken their faith, and where the greatest advantages have failed to induce republics to disregard theirs . . . I do not speak of the breaking of treaties because of an occasional non-observance, that being an ordinary matter; but I speak of the breaking of treaties from some extraordinary cause; and here I believe, from what has been said, that the people are less frequently guilty of this than princes, and are therefore more to be trusted. (*D*, I:59)

[With] no adequate remedies existing for . . . disorders arising in republics, it follows that it is impossible to establish a perpetual republic, because in a thousand unforeseen ways its ruin may be accomplished. (*D*, III:17)

[V]ery often actions that seem good on the surface, and which cannot reasonably be objected to, may become oppressive and highly dangerous to a republic unless they are corrected betimes. To explain this matter more fully, I say that a republic that has no distinguished citizens cannot be well-governed; but, on the other hand, it is often the great influence of such distinguished citizens that is the cause of states being reduced to servitude. And to prevent this the institutions of the state should be so regulated that the influence of citizens shall be founded only upon such acts as are of benefit to the state, and not upon such as are injurious to the public interests or liberty. And therefore attention must be given to the means employed by citizens for acquiring such influence; and these are twofold, either public or private. The former are when a citizen gains reputation and influence by serving the state well with his counsels or his actions. The way to such honors should be open to every citizen, and suitable rewards should be established that will be satisfactory and honorable to those who merit them. Reputation and influence gained by such pure and simple means will never prove dangerous to any state. But when they are acquired by private means, then they become most dangerous and pernicious. These private ways consist in benefiting this or the other private individual, by lending them money, marrying their daughters, sustaining them against the authority of the magistrates, and bestowing upon them such other favors as to make partisans of them. This encourages those who are thus favored to corrupt the public and to outrage the laws. A well-regulated republic, therefore, should open the way to public honors to those who seek reputation by means that are conducive to the public good; and close it to those whose aim is the advancement of private ends. It was thus that Rome decreed the reward of triumphs and other honors to such of her citizens as had acted well for the public good; while, on the other hand, she ordered accusations to be brought against those who under various pretexts aimed to make themselves powerful for private ends. And when such accusations did not suffice, in consequence of the people's being blinded by a sort of false and illusory advantage, they created a Dictator, who, armed with regal powers, caused them to return to the true path of duty from which they had strayed . . . And if one such transgression were allowed to go unpunished, it might lead to the ruin of the republic, for it would then be difficult to force back the ambitious to the true path of duty. (*D*, III:28)

[I]t is not good that one kind of magistrate or council should be able to retard public business without someone's being there who can arrange for action. It is also not good that officeholders should not have somebody to observe them and make them abstain from actions that are not good. (*GF*)

The reason why Florence throughout her history has frequently varied her methods of government is that she has never been either a republic or a princedom having the qualities each requires, because we cannot call that republic well-established in which things are done according to the will of one man yet are decided with the approval of many; nor can we believe a republic fitted to last, in which there is no contentment for those elements that must be contented if republics are not to fall. (*GF*)

There is no other way of escaping these ills than to give the city institutions that can by themselves stand firm. And they will always stand firm when everybody has a hand in them, and when everybody knows what he needs to do and in whom he can trust, and no class of citizen, either through fear for itself or through ambition, will need to desire revolution. (*GF*)

[I]t has been observed by the Magnificent and Exalted Signors [of Florence] that all republics which in times past have preserved and increased themselves have always had as their chief basis two things, to wit, justice and arms, in order to restrain and to govern their subjects, and in order to defend themselves from their enemies. (*PI*)

There will always be a greater number of excellent men in republics than in monarchies because *virtù* is generally honored in the former, but feared in the latter; hence, it comes to pass that men of *virtù* are cherished and encouraged in one, but discountenanced and suppressed in the other. (*AW*, 2)

IV. Religion and the State

Although the founder of Rome was Romulus, to whom like a daughter, she owed her birth and her education, yet the gods did not judge the laws of this prince sufficient for so great an empire, and therefore inspired the Roman Senate to elect Numa Pompilius as his successor, so that he might regulate all those things that had been omitted by Romulus. Numa, finding a very savage people, and wishing to reduce them to civil obedience by the arts or peace, had recourse to religion as the most necessary and assured support of any civil society; and he established it upon such foundations that for many centuries there was nowhere more fear of the gods than in that republic, which greatly facilitated all the enterprises which the Senate or its great men attempted. Whoever will examine the actions of the people of Rome as a body, or of many individual Romans, will see that these citizens feared much more to break an oath than the laws; like men who esteem the power of the gods more than that of men. . . . And whoever reads Roman history attentively will see in how great a degree religion served in the command of the armies, in uniting the people and keeping them well-conducted, and in covering the wicked with shame. So that if the question were discussed whether Rome was more indebted to Romulus or to Numa, I believe that the highest merit would be conceded to Numa; for where religion exists it is easy to introduce armies and discipline, but where there are armies and no religion it is difficult to introduce the latter. . . . In truth, there never was any remarkable lawgiver amongst any people who did not resort to divine authority, as otherwise his laws would not have been accepted by the people; for there are many good laws, the importance of which is known to the sagacious lawgiver, but the reasons for which are not sufficiently evident to enable him to persuade others to submit to them; and therefore do wise men, for the purpose of removing this difficulty, resort to divine authority. Thus did Lycurgus and Solon, and many others who aimed at the same thing.

The Roman people, then, admiring the wisdom and goodness of Numa, yielded in all things to his advice. It is true that those were very religious times, and the people with whom Numa had to deal were very untutored and superstitious, which made it easy for him to carry out his designs, being able to impress upon them any new form. And doubtless, if anyone wanted to establish a republic at the present time, he would find it much

easier with the simple mountaineers, who are almost without any civilization, than with such as are accustomed to live in cities, where civilization
is already corrupt; as a sculptor finds it easier to make a fine statue out of
a crude block of marble than of a statue badly begun by another. Considering, then, all these things, I conclude that the religion introduced by Numa
into Rome was one of the chief causes of the prosperity of that city; for
this religion gave rise to good laws, and good laws bring good fortune, and
from good fortune results happy successes in all enterprises. And as the
observance of divine institutions is the cause of the greatness of republics,
so the disregard of them produces their ruin; for where the fear of God is
wanting, there the country will come to ruin, unless it is sustained by the
fear of the prince, which may temporarily supply the want of religion. But
as the lives of princes are short, the kingdom will of necessity perish as the
prince fails in virtue. Whence it comes that kingdoms which depend
entirely upon the virtue of one man endure but for a brief time, for his
virtue passes away with his life, and it rarely happens that it is renewed in
his successor, as Dante so wisely says:

"Tis seldom human wisdom descends from sire to son;
    Such is the will of Him who gave it,
    That at his hands alone we may implore the boon."

The welfare, then, of a republic or a kingdom does not consist in
having a prince who governs it wisely during his lifetime, but in having
one who will give it such laws that it will maintain itself even after his
death. And although untutored and ignorant men are more easily
persuaded to adopt new laws or new opinions, yet that does not make it
impossible to persuade civilized men who claim to be enlightened. (*D*,
I:11)

Princes and republics who wish to maintain themselves free from corruption must above all things preserve the purity of all religious observances,
and treat them with proper reverence; for there is no greater indication of
the ruin of a country than to see religion contemned. And this is easily
understood, when we know upon what the religion of a country is founded;
for the essence of every religion is based upon some one main principle.
(*D*, I:12)

It is therefore the duty of princes and heads of republics to uphold the
foundations of the religion of their countries, for then it is easy to keep
their people religious, and consequently well-conducted and united. And
therefore everything that tends to favor religion (even though it were

believed to be false) should be received and availed of to strengthen it; and this should be done the more, the wiser the rulers are, and the better they understand the natural course of things. Such was, in fact, the practice observed by sagacious men; which has given rise to the belief in the miracles that are celebrated in religions, however false they may be. For the sagacious rulers have given these miracles increased importance, no matter whence or how they originated; and their authority afterwards gave them credence with the people. (*D*, I:12)

In Germany alone do we see that probity and religion still largely amongst the people, in consequence of which many republics exist there in the full enjoyment of liberty, observing their laws in such a manner that no one from within or without could venture upon an attempt to master them. (*D*, I:55)

Reflecting now as to whence it came that in ancient times the people were more devoted to liberty than in the present, I believe that it resulted from this, that men were stronger in those days, which I believe to be attributable to the difference of education, founded upon the difference of their religion and ours. For as our religion teaches us the truth and the true way of life, it causes us to attach less value to the honors and possessions of this world; while the Pagans, esteeming those things as the highest good, were more energetic and ferocious in their actions. We may observe this also in most of their institutions, beginning with the magnificence of their sacrifices as compared with the humility of ours, which are gentle solemnities rather than magnificent ones, and have nothing of energy or ferocity in them, while in theirs there was no lack of pomp and show, to which was superadded the ferocious and bloody nature of the sacrifice by the slaughter of many animals; and the familiarity with this terrible sight assimilated the nature of men to their sacrificial ceremonies. Besides this, the Pagan religion deified only men who achieved great glory, such as commanders of armies and chiefs of republics, while ours glorifies more humble and contemplative men than the men of action. Our religion, moreover, places the supreme happiness in humility, lowliness, and a contempt for worldly objects, while the other, on the contrary, places the supreme good in grandeur of soul, strength of body, and all such other qualities as render men formidable. And if our religion claims of us fortitude of soul, it is more to enable us to suffer than to achieve great deeds.

These principles seem to me to have made men feeble, and caused them to become an easy prey to evil-minded men who can control them more securely, seeing that the great body of men, for sake of gaining Paradise, are more disposed to endure injuries than to avenge them. And although it would seem that the world has become effeminate and Heaven disarmed, yet this arises unquestionably from the baseness of men, who have interpreted our religion according to the promptings of indolence rather than those of virtue. For if we were to reflect that our religion permits us to exalt and defend our country, we should see that according to it we ought also to love and honor our country, and prepare ourselves so as to be capable of defending her. It is this education, then, and this false interpretation of our religion, that is the cause of there not being so many republics nowadays as there were in ancient times; and that there is no longer the same love of liberty amongst the people now as there was then. (*D*, II:2)

Religion, too, and the oath [Roman] soldiers took when they were enlisted, greatly contributed to making them do their duty in ancient times; for upon any default, they were threatened not only with human punishments, but the vengeance of the gods. They also had several other religious ceremonies that had a very good effect on all their enterprises, and would still have in any place where religion is held in reverence. (*AW*, IV)

V. Citizens, Classes, and Faction

I maintain that, those who blame the quarrels of the Senate and the people of Rome, condemn that which was the very origin of liberty, and that they were probably more impressed by the cries and noise which these disturbances occasioned in the public places, than by the good effect which they produced; and that they do not consider that in every republic there are two parties, that of the nobles and that of the people; and all the laws that are favorable to liberty result from the opposition of these parties to each other, as may easily be seen from the events that occurred in Rome. From the time of the Tarquins to that of the Gracchi, that is to say, within the space of over three hundred years, the differences between these parties caused but very few exiles, and cost still less blood; they cannot therefore be regarded as having been very injurious and fatal to a republic, which during the course of so many years saw on this account only eight or ten of its citizens sent into exile, and but a very small number put to death, and even but a few condemned to pecuniary fines. Nor can we regard a republic as disorderly where so many virtues were seen to shine. For good examples are the result of good education, and good education is due to good laws; and good laws in their turn spring from those very agitations which have been so inconsiderably condemned by many. For whoever will carefully examine the result of these agitations will find that they have neither caused exiles nor any violence prejudicial to the general good, and will be convinced even that they have given rise to laws that were to the advantage of public liberty. And if it be said that these are strange means -- to hear constantly the cries of the people furious against the Senate, and of a Senate declaiming against the people, to see the populace rush tumultuously through the streets, close their houses, and even leave the city of Rome -- I reply that all these things can alarm only those who read of them, and that every state ought to afford the people the opportunity of giving vent, so to say, to their ambition; and above all those republics which on important occasions have to avail themselves of this very people. Now such were the means employed at Rome; when the people wanted to obtain a law they resorted to some of the extremes of which we have just spoken, or they refused to enroll themselves to serve in the wars, so that the Senate was obliged to satisfy them in some measure. The demands of a free people are rarely pernicious to their liberty; they are generally inspired by oppressions, experienced or apprehended; and if their fears are ill-founded, resort is had to public assemblies where the mere eloquence of a single good and respectable man will make them sensible of their error. "The people," says Cicero, "although ignorant, yet are capable of appreciating the truth, and yield to it readily when it is presented to them by a man whom they esteem worthy of their confidence."

One should show then more reserve in blaming the Roman government, and consider that so many good effects, which originated in that republic, cannot but result from very good causes. If the troubles of Rome occasioned the creation of Tribunes, then they cannot be praised too highly; for besides giving to the people a share in the public administration, these Tribunes were established as the most assured guardians of Roman liberty . . . (*D*, I:4)

[A]s the vice of ingratitude is usually the consequence of either avarice or fear, it will be seen that the peoples never fall into this error from avarice, and that fear also makes them less liable to it than princes, inasmuch as they have less reason for fear . . . (*D*, I:29)

[T]he ambition of the nobles is so great that, if it is not repressed by various ways and means in any city, it will quickly bring that city to ruin. (*D*, I:37)

It seems . . . that [great troubles] are more frequently occasioned by those who possess; for the fear to lose stirs the same passions in men as the desire to gain, as men do not believe themselves sure of what they already possess except by acquiring still more; and, moreover, these new acquisitions are so many means of strength and power for abusers; and what is still worse is that the haughty manners and insolence of the nobles and the rich excite in the breasts of those who have neither birth nor wealth, not only the desire to possess them, but also the wish to revenge themselves by depriving the former of those riches and honors which they see them employ so badly. (*D*, I:5)

As every [ancient] republic was composed of nobles and people, the question arose as to whose hands it was best to confide the protection of liberty. The Spartans, and in our day the Venetians, gave it into the hands of the nobility; but the Romans intrusted it to the people. We must examine, therefore, which of these republics made the best choice. There are strong reasons in favor of each, but to judge by the results we must incline in favor of the nobles, for the liberties of Sparta and Venice endured a longer space than those of Rome. But to come to the reasons, taking the part of Rome first, I will say that one should always confide any deposit to those who have least desire of violating it; and doubtless, if we consider the objects of the nobles and of the people, we must see that the first have a great desire to dominate, while the latter have only the wish not to be dominated, and consequently a greater desire to live in the enjoyment of liberty; so that when the people are entrusted with the care of any privilege or liberty, being less disposed to encroach upon it, they will of necessity take better care of it; and being unable to take it away themselves, will prevent others from doing so.

On the contrary, it is said in favor of the course adopted by Sparta and Venice, that the preference given to the nobility, as guardians of public liberty, has two advantages; the first, to yield something to the ambition of those who, being more engaged in the management of public affairs, find, so to say, in the weapon which the office places in their hands, a means of power that satisfies them; the other, to deprive the restless spirit of the massses of an authority calculated from its very nature to produce trouble and dissensions, apt to drive the nobles to some act of desperation, which in time may cause the greatest misfortunes. Rome is even adduced as an example of this; for having confided, it is said, this authority to the Tribunes of the people, these were seen not to be content with having only one Consul taken from this class, but wanted both to be plebeians. They afterwards claimed the Censorship, the Praetoriate, and all the other dignities of the republic. And not satisfied with these advantages, and urged on by the same violence, they came in the end to idolize all those whom they saw disposed to attack the nobles, which gave rise to the power of Marius and to the ruin of Rome. And, truly, whoever weighs all these reasons accurately may well remain in doubt which of the two classes he would choose as the guardians of liberty, not knowing which would be least dangerous; those who seek to acquire an authority which they have not, or those who desire to preserve that which they already possess. After the nicest examination, this is what I think may be concluded from it. The question refers either to a republic that desires to extend its empire, as Rome, or to a state that confines itself merely to its own preservation. In the first case Rome should be imitated, and in the second the example of Sparta and Venice should be followed . . . (*D*, I:5)

[A]n offense of private individuals against a private individual, which kind of offenses generate fear, and fear seeks for means of defense, and for that purpose seeks partisans, and from partisans arise factions in cities, and factions cause their ruin. (*D*, I:7)

[W]e may conclude that, whenever the aid of foreign powers is called in by any party in a state, it is to be ascribed to defects in the constitution, and more especially to the want of means for enabling the people to exhaust the malign humors that spring up among men, without having recourse to extraordinary measures; all of which can easily be provided against by instituting accusations before numerous judges, and giving these sufficient influence and importance. These things were so well-organized in Rome that, with the many dissensions between the Senate and the people, neither the one nor the other, nor any private citizen, ever attempted to avail of foreign force; for having the remedy at home, there was no occasion to look for it elsewhere. (*D*, I:7)

But if the people had been corrupt, then there would have been no sufficient remedies found in Rome or elsewhere to maintain their liberty. (*D*, I:16)

[W]e may draw the conclusion that, where the mass of the people is sound, disturbances and tumults do no serious harm; but where corruption has penetrated the people, the best laws are of no avail, unless they are administered by a man of such supreme power that he may cause the laws to be observed until the mass has been restored to a healthy condition. And I know not whether such a case has ever occurred, or whether it possibly ever could occur. . . . For if a state or city in decadence, in consequence of the corruption of the mass of its people, is ever raised up again, it must be through the virtue of some one man then living, and not by the people; and so soon as such a man dies, the people will relapse into their corrupt habits . . . And the reason of this is that one man cannot live long enough to have time to bring a people back to good habits which for any length of time has indulged in evil ones. Or if one of extreme long life, or two continuous virtuous successors, do not restore the state, it will quickly lapse into ruin, no matter how many dangers and how much bloodshed have been incurred in the effort to restore it. For such corruption and incapacity to maintain free institutions result from a great inequality that exists in such a state; and to reduce the inhabitants to equality requires the application of extraordinary measures, which few know how, or are willing to employ. (*D*, I:17)

And as I have demonstrated elsewhere that the differences between the Senate and the people had been instrumental in preserving liberty in Rome, because they had given rise to the enactment of laws favorable to liberty, therefore the results of this agrarian law [which sought to redistribute land] may seem to be in contradiction with that previous conclusion.

But I do not on that account change my opinion, for the ambition of the nobles is so great, that if it is not repressed by various ways and means in any city, it will quickly bring that city to ruin. So that if the contentions about the agrarian law needed three hundred years to bring Rome to a state of servitude, she would have been brought there much quicker if the people, by these laws and other means, had not for so great a length of time kept the ambition of the nobles in check. (*D*, I:37)

[T]he necessity of creating the tyranny of the Decemvirs in Rome arose from the same causes that generally produce tyrannies in cities; that is to say, the too great desire of the people to be free, and the equally too great desire of the nobles to dominate. And if the two parties do not agree to secure liberty by law, and either the one or the other throws all its influence in favor of one man, then a tyranny is the natural result. (*D*, I:40)

For with the support of the people [a tyrant] will be enabled to destroy the nobility, and after these are crushed he will not fail in turn to crush the people; and by the time they become sensible of their own enslavement, they will have no one to look to for succor. This is the course which all those have followed who have imposed tyrannies upon republics. (*D*, I:40)

Reflecting now upon all that has been said, we see that the quickest way of opening the eyes of the people is to find the means of making them descend to particulars, seeing that to look at things only in a general way deceives them . . . I believe also that we may conclude from it that no wise man should ever disregard the popular judgment upon particular matters, such as the distribution of honors and dignities; for in these things the people never deceive themselves, or if they do, it is much less frequently than a small body would do who had been especially charged with such distributions. (*D*, I:47)

Here we have to note two things; first, that the people often, deceived by an illusive good, desire their own ruin, and unless they are made sensible of the evil of the one and the benefit of the other course by someone in whom they have confidence, they will expose the republic to infinite peril and damage. And if it happens that the people have no confidence in anyone, as sometimes will be the case when they have been deceived before by events or men, then it will inevitably lead to the ruin of the state. Dante says upon this point in his discourse "On Monarchy," that the people often shout, "Life to our death, and death to our life!" It is this want of confidence on the part of the people that causes good measures to be often rejected in republics. (*D*, I:53)

If we consider now what is easy and what is difficult to persuade a people to, we may make this distinction: either what you wish to persuade them to represents at first sight gain or loss, or it seems brave or cowardly. And if you propose to them anything that upon its face seems profitable and courageous, though there be really a loss concealed under it which may involve the ruin of the republic, the multitude will ever be most easily persuaded to it. But if the measure proposed seems doubtful and likely to cause loss, then it will be difficult to persuade the people to it, even though the benefit and welfare of the republic were concealed under it. All this is supported by numerous examples amongst the Romans as well as strangers, and both in modern and in ancient times. (*D*, I:53)

I say that there is no easier way to ruin a republic where the people have power, than to involve them in daring enterprises; for where the people have influence they will always be ready to engage in them, and no contrary opinion will prevent them. But if such enterprises cause the ruin of states, they still more frequently cause the ruin of the particular citizens who are placed at the head to conduct them. For when defeat comes, instead of the successors which the people expected, they charge it neither upon the ill fortune or incompetence of their leaders, but upon their wickedness and ignorance; and generally to many Carthaginian and Athenian generals. Their previous victories are of no advantage to them, for they are all canceled by present defeat. (*D*, I:53)

Titus Livius as well as all other historians affirm that nothing is more uncertain and inconstant than the multitude; for it appears from what he relates of the actions of men, that in many instances the multitude, after having condemned a man to death, bitterly lamented it, and most earnestly wished him back. (*D*, I:58)

[B]ut [kings controlled by the law] should be compared with a people equally controlled by the law . . . and then we shall find in that multitude the same good qualities as in those kings, and we shall see that such a people neither obey with servility nor command with insolence. Such were the people of Rome, who so long as that republic remained uncorrupted, neither obeyed basely nor ruled insolently, but rather held its rank honorably, supporting the laws and their magistrates. And when the unrighteous ambition of some noble made it necessary for them to rise up in self-defense, they did so . . . (*D*, I:58)

But what our historian [Livy] says of the character of the multitude does not apply to a people regulated by laws, as the Romans were, but to an unbridled multitude, such as the Syracusans; who committed all the excessses to which infuriated and unbridled men abandon themselves, as did Alexander the Great and Herod . . .Therefore the character of the people is not to be blamed any more than that of princes, for both alike are liable to err when they are without any control. (*D*, I:58)

Contrary to the general opinion . . . which maintains that the people, when they govern, are inconsistent, unstable, and ungrateful, I conclude and affirm that these defects are not more natural to the people than they are to princes. To charge the people and princes equally with them may be the truth, but to except princes from them would be a great mistake. For a people that governs and is well-regulated by laws will be stable, prudent, and grateful, as much so, and even more, according to my opinion, than a prince, although he be esteemed wise; and, on the other hand, a prince, freed from the restraints of the law, will be more ungrateful, inconstant, and imprudent than a people similarly situated. The difference in their conduct is not due to any difference in their nature (for it is the same, and if there be any difference for good, it is on the side of the people), but to the greater or less respect they have for the laws under which they respectively live. (*D*, I:58)

[T]he people are less ungrateful than princes, but as regards prudence and stability, I say that the people are more prudent and stable, and have better judgment than a prince; and it is not without good reason that it is said, "The voice of the people is the voice of God;" for we see popular opinion prognosticate events in such a wonderful manner that it would almost seem as if the people had some occult virtue, which enables them to foresee the good and the evil. As to the people's capacity of judging of things, it is exceedingly rare that, when they hear two orators of equal talents advocate different measures, they do not decide in favor of the best of the two, which proves their ability to discern the truth of what they hear. And if occasionally they are mislead in matters involving questions of courage or seeming utility, as has been shown, so is a prince also many times misled by his own passions, which are much greater than those of the people. We also see that in the election of their magistrates they make far better choice than princes; and no people will ever be persuaded to elect a man of infamous character and corrupt habits to any post of dignity, to which a prince is easily influenced in a thousand different ways. When we see a people take an aversion to anything, they persist in it for many centuries, which we never find to be the case with princes. Upon both these points the Roman people shall serve me as a proof, who in the many elections of Consuls and Tribunes had to regret only four times the choice they had made. The Roman people held the name of king in such detestation, as we have said, that no extent of services rendered by any of its citizens who attempted to usurp that title could save him from his merited punishment. We furthermore see the cities where the people are masters make the greatest progress in the least possible time, and much greater than such as have always been governed by princes; as was the case with Rome after the expulsion of the kings, and with Athens after they rid themselves of Pisistratus; and this can be attributed to no other cause than that the governments of the people are better than those of princes. . . .

[F]or if we compare the faults of a people with those of princes, as well as their respective good qualities, we shall find the people vastly superior in all that is good and glorious. And if princes show themselves superior in the making of laws, and in the forming of civil institutions and new statutes and ordinances, the people are superior in maintaining those institutions, laws, and ordinances, which certainly places them on a par with those who established them.

And finally to sum up this matter, I say that both governments of princes and of the people have lasted a long time, but both required to be regulated by laws. For a prince who knows no other control but his own will is like a madman, and a people that can do as it pleases will hardly be wise. If now we compare a prince who is controlled by laws, and a people that is untrammeled by them, we shall find more virtue in the people than in the prince; and if we compare them when both are freed from such control, we shall see that the people are guilty of fewer excesses than the prince, and that the errors of the people are of less importance, and therefore more easily remedied. For a licentious and mutinous people may easily be brought back to good conduct by the influence and persuasion of a good man, but an evil-minded prince is not amenable to such influences, and therefore there is no other remedy against him but cold steel. We may judge, then, from this of the relative defects of the one and the other; if words suffice to correct those of the people, while those of the prince can only be remedied by violence, no one can fail to see that where the greater remedy is required, there also the defects must be greater. The follies which a people commits at the moment of its greatest license are not what is most to be feared; it is not the immediate evil that may result from them that inspires apprehension, but the fact that such general confusion might afford the opportunity for a tyrant to seize the government. But with evil-disposed princes the contrary is the case; it is the immediate present that causes fear, and there is hope only in the future; for men will persuade themselves that the termination of his wicked life may give them a chance of liberty. Thus we see the difference between the one and the other to be, that the one touches the present and the other the future. The excesses of the people are directed against those whom they suspect of interfering with the public good, while those of princes are against apprehended interference with their individual interests. The general prejudice against the people results from the fact that everybody can freely and fearlessly speak ill of them in mass, even while they are at the height of their power; but a prince can only be spoken of with the greatest circumspection and apprehension. (*D*, I:58)

[T]he people will avenge their lost liberty with more energy than when it is merely threatened. (*D*, II:2)

It has ever been, and ever will be the case that men of rare and extraordinary merit are neglected by republics in times of peace and tranquillity; for jealous of the reputation which such men have acquired by their virtues, there are always in such times many other citizens who want to be not only their equals, but their superiors. (*D*, III:16)

I will show how nothing is to be gained by attempting to control cities by means of keeping alive factions. For it is impossible either for a prince or a republic to preserve an equal influence over both the old factions, it being in the nature of man in all differences of opinion to prefer either the one side of the other. Thus, one of the parties being malcontent, you will lose the city on the occasion of the first war, it being impossible to hold it against enemies from without and within. If the government of the city is a republic, then there is no surer way of corrupting the citizens and to divide the city against itself, than to foment the spirit of faction that may prevail there; for each party will strive by every means of corruption to secure friends and supporters, which gives rise to two most serious evils: first, that a government which changes, often according to the caprice of the one or the other faction, can never be good, and consequently never can secure to itself the good will and attachment of its citizens; and, secondly, that such favoring of factions keeps the republic of necessity divided. (*D*, III:27)

[T]he people show more wisdom in their selection [of public officers] than princes. I say, then, that the people are guided in their choice either by what is said of a man by the public voice and fame, even if by his open acts he appears different, or by the preconceptions or opinion which they may have formed of him themselves. And these are based either upon the character of the fathers of such men, who were so eminent and influential in the republic that the people suppose the sons will be like them unless by their actions they have given proof of the contrary, or that opinion is founded upon the individual conduct of the parties in question. The best means of judging of this is to ascertain whether they choose for their companions men of known respectability, good habits, and generally well-reputed. For there is no better indication of a man's character than the company which he keeps; and therefore very properly a man who keeps respectable company acquires a good name, for it is impossible that there should not be some similitude of character and habits between him and his associates. Or indeed a man acquires this good reputation by some extraordinary act, which, although relating to private matters, will still obtain him celebrity if it be honorably performed. And of these three things that give a man a good reputation, the last is the most influential. For the first, being founded upon the merits of a man's father or relations, is so fallacious that it makes no lasting impression and is soon effaced altogether, unless sustained by the individual merits of him who has to be judged. The second, which makes a man known by the company he keeps, and by his social conduct is better than the first, but inferior to that which is founded upon his individual actions; for unless a man has by these given some proof of himself, his reputation will depend merely upon public opinion, which is most unstable. But the third course, being founded entirely upon a man's own actions, will from the start give him such a name that it will require a long course of opposite conduct to destroy it. Men who are born in a republic, therefore, should adopt this last course, and strive to distinguish themselves by some remarkable action.

This is what many of the young men of Rome did, either by proposing some law that was for the general good, or by preferring charges against some powerful citizen as a transgressor of the laws; or by some similar and novel act that would cause them to be talked about. Such conduct is necessary not only for the purpose of achieving a name and fame, but also to preserve and increase it. To do this requires a frequent repetition of similar acts . . . Such conduct is necessary not only for those citizens who desire to achieve distinction for the purpose of obtaining honorable employment in their republics, but equally so for princes to enable them to maintain their dignity and reputation in their dominions. For nothing so certainly secures to a prince the public esteem as some such remarkable action or saying dictated by his regard for the public good, showing him to be magnanimous, liberal, and just, and which action or saying is of a nature to become familiar as a proverb amongst his subjects. But to return to our first proposition, I say that when the people begin to bestow office upon a citizen, influenced thereto by the three above given reasons, they act wisely. They do still better, however, when they base their choice upon a number of good actions known to have been performed by him; for in that case they are never deceived. I speak only of such offices and grades as

are given to men in the beginning before they have established their reputation by confirmed experience, and before they have time to fall into an
opposite course of conduct. Thus the people are always less liable to the
influence of erroneous opinions and corruption than princes; although it
might happen that the people are deceived by public opinion and the fame
and acts of a man, supposing him to be better than he really is, which
would not happen to a prince, who would be informed of it by his coun-
selors. Therefore, so that the people might not lack similar counsel, the
wise lawgivers of republics have ordered that in the appointment of men
to the highest positions, where it would be dangerous to place inefficient
persons, every citizen should be allowed, and in fact it should be
accounted honorable for him, to publish in the assemblies the defects of
anyone named to public office; so that the people, fully informed, might
form a more correct judgment. . . . The people then are influenced in the
choice of their magistrates by the best evidences they can obtain of the
qualifications of the candidates, and are less liable to error than princes
when equally counseled. Every citizen, therefore, who desires to win the
favor of the people, should strive to merit it by some notable action . . . (*D*,
III:34)

The reason why all these [Florentine] governments have been defective is
that the alterations in them have been made not for the fulfillment of the
common good, but for the strengthening and security of the party making
them. Such security has not yet been attained, because there has always
been in the city a party that was discontented, which has been a very
powerful tool for anybody who wished to make a change. (*GF*)

If any reading is useful to citizens who govern republics, it is that which
shows the causes of the hatreds and factional struggles within the city, in
order that such citizens, having grown wise through the sufferings of
others, can keep themselves united.
    If the experiences of any republic are moving, those of a man's own
city, when he reads about them, are much more moving and more useful;
and if in any republic internal dissensions were ever worth noting, in that
of Florence they are especially noteworthy, because most of the other
republics of which there is any record have been content with one sort of
factional struggle, with which, according as it has happened, they have
sometimes expanded, sometimes ruined their cities. But Florence, not
content with one sort of factional quarrel has had many. In Rome, as
everybody knows, after the kings were driven out, there was disunion
between the nobles and the people, which continued in the city until her
fall. So it did in Athens, and in all the other republics that flourished in

those days. But in Florence, first there were factions among the nobles, then factional struggles between the nobles and the middle class, finally between the middle class and the masses. Many times it happened that one of these parties, having conquered the others, was itself divided into two factions. From these dissensions resulted as many deaths, as many exiles, as many ruined families as ever were known in any city of which we have record. Certainly, according to my judgment, nothing shows so well the vigor of our city as does the quality of these dissensions, which had might enough to destroy the greatest and most powerful of cities. Nevertheless, ours seemed always to grow stronger. Such was the ability of those citizens and the power of their intelligence and spirit to make themselves and their native city great, that as many as remained superior to so many ills could do more to exalt her with their ability than the evil influence of those events that might have weakened her could do to depress her. And beyond doubt if Florence had had the good fortune, when she freed herself from the [Roman] Empire, to take a form of government that would have kept her united, I do not know what republic, modern or ancient, would have been superior to her -- with such ability in arms and in peaceful arts she would have abounded. (*HF*, preface)

Those cities, especially such as are not well-organized, that are administered under the semblance of republican government, often vary their rulers and their constitutions not between liberty and slavery, as many believe, but between slavery and license. The promoters of license, who are the people, and the promoters of slavery, who are the nobles, praise the mere name of liberty, for neither of these classes is willing to be subject either to the laws or to men. I allow that when it comes about (and it seldom does come about) that by a city's good fortune a wise, good, and powerful citizen gains power who establishes laws that repress strife between the nobles and the people, or so restrain these parties that they cannot do evil, at such a time a city can be called free and her government can be considered firm and solid; being founded on good laws and good institutions, it does not need, as do other governments, the strength and wisdom of one man to maintain it.

With such laws and institutions many ancient republics, whose governments had long lives, were gifted. Such customs and laws have been wanting to all those which have often varied their governments and are at present varying them from the tyrannical form to the licentious, and from that back to the other; on account of the powerful enemies both have, they are not and cannot be stable. The tyrannical form does not satisfy good men; the licentious dissatisfies the wise. The first can do evil with ease; the second can do good with difficulty. In one, too much power is given to arrogant men; in the other, too much to stupid men. Either one has to be maintained by the ability and the good fortune of a single man, who may be removed by death or become incompetent through disease. (*HF*, IV:1)

[A]ccording to my habit, I wish to some extent to explain in general why those who believe republics can be united are greatly deceived in their belief. It is true that some divisions harm republics and some divisions benefit them. Those do harm that are accompanied with factions and partisans; those bring benefit that are kept up without factions and without partisans. Since, then, the founder of a republic cannot provide that there will be no enmities within it, he needs at least to provide that there will be no factions. Therefore he must note that in two ways citizens gain reputation in a city: activity in behalf of the public, and activity for personal ends. Publicly they gain reputation by winning a battle, capturing a town, carrying on an embassy with diligence and prudence, and advising the state wisely and successfully. In personal ways they gain reputation by doing favors to various citizens, defending them from the magistrates, assisting them with money and aiding them in getting undeserved offices, and by pleasing the masses with games and public gifts. From these selfish proceedings come factions and partisans; a reputation so gained injures the state. Yet a reputation gained by unselfish conduct benefits the republic, since it is not mixed with partisanship, being founded on the common good, not on private favor. Even citizens who confer private benefits cannot harm the republic unless they have partisans who follow them for personal profit, though no one can in any way provide against their exciting great hatred. When they have no partisans, even selfishly ambitious men benefit the state, because if they are to succeed, necessarily they attempt to make the republic great, and especially watch each other in order that lawful bounds may not be overpassed. (*HF*, VII:1)

VI. The Roman Paradigm

The example of Rome is preferable to all others. (*D*, I:17)

[N]either the fertility of the soil, the proximity of the sea, nor their many victories, nor the greatness of their empire, could corrupt [the Romans] during several centuries, and they maintained there more virtues than have ever been seen in any other republic. (*D*, I:1)

I believe it will not be amiss to consider whether in a state that has become corrupt, a free government that has existed there can be maintained; or if there has been none before, whether one could be established there. Upon this subject I must say that either one of them would be exceedingly difficult. And although it is impossible to give any definite rules for such a case (as it will be necessary to proceed according to the different degrees of corruption), yet as it is well to reason upon all subjects, I will not leave this problem without discussing it. I will suppose a state to be corrupt to the last degree, so as to present the subject in its most difficult aspect, there being no laws nor institutions that suffice to check a general corruption. For as good habits of the people require good laws to support them, so laws, to be observed, need good habits on the part of the people. Besides, the constitutions and the laws established in a republic at its very origin when men were still pure, no longer suit when men have become corrupt and bad. And although the laws may be changed according to circumstances and events, yet it is seldom or never that the constitution itself is changed; and for this reason the new laws do not suffice, for they are not in harmony with the constitution, that has remained intact. To make this matter better understood, I will explain how the government of Rome was constituted and what the nature of the laws was, which together with the magistrates restrained the citizens. The constitution of the state reposed upon the authority of the people, the Senate, the Tribunes, and the Consuls, and upon the manner of choosing and creating the magistrates, and of making the laws. These institutions were rarely or never varied by events; but the laws that restrained the citizens were often altered, such as the law relating to adultery, the sumptuary laws, that in relation to ambition, and many others, which were changed according as the citizens from one day to another became more and more corrupt. Now the constitution remaining unchanged, although no longer suitable to the corrupt people, the laws that had been changed became powerless for restraint; yet they would have answered very well if the constitution had also been modified at the same time with the laws.

And the truth that the original institutions were no longer suitable to a corrupt state is clearly seen in these two main points -- the creation of the magistrates, and the forms used in making the laws. As regards the first, the Roman people bestowed the Consulate and the other principal offices only on such as asked for them. This system was very good in the beginning, because only such citizens asked for these places as deemed themselves worthy of them, and a refusal was regarded as ignominious; so that everyone strove to make himself esteemed worthy of the honor. But when the city had become corrupt, this system became most pernicious; for it was no longer the most virtuous and deserving, but the most powerful that asked for the magistracies; and the less powerful, often the most meritorious, abstained from being candidates from fear. This state of things did not come all at once, but by degrees, as is generally the case with other vices. For after the Romans had subjected Africa and Asia, and had reduced nearly all Greece to their obedience, they felt assured of their liberty, and saw no enemies that could cause them any apprehension. This security and the weakness of the conquered nations caused the Roman people no longer to bestow the consulate according to the merits of the candidates, but according to favor; giving that dignity to those who best knew how to entertain the people, and not to those who best knew how to conquer their enemies. After that they descended from those who were most favored to such as had most wealth and power, so that the really meritorious became wholly excluded from that dignity. Now as to the mode of making the laws. At first a Tribune or any other citizen had the right to propose any law, and every citizen could speak in favor or against it before its final adoption. This system was very good so long as the citizens were uncorrupted, for it is always well in a state that everyone may propose what he deems for the public good; and it was equally well that every one should be allowed to express his opinion in relation to it, so that the people, having heard both sides, may decide in favor of the best. But when the citizens had become corrupt, this system became the worst possible, for then only the powerful proposed laws, not for the common good and the liberty of all, but for the increase of their own power, and fear restrained all the others from speaking against such laws, and thus the people were by force and fraud made to resolve upon their own ruin.

It was necessary, therefore, if Rome wished to preserve her liberty in the midst of this corruption, that she should have modified her constitution, in like manner as in the progress of her existence she had made new laws; for institutions and forms should be adopted to the subject, whether it be good or evil, inasmuch as the same form cannot suit two subjects that are essentially different. But as the constitution of a state, when once it has been discovered to be no longer suitable, should be amended, either all at once, or by degrees as each defect becomes known, I say that both of these courses are equally impossible. For a gradual modification requires to be the work of some wise man, who has seen the evil from afar in its very beginning; but it is very likely that such a man may never rise up in the state, and even if he did he will hardly be able to persuade the others to what he proposes; for men accustomed to live after one fashion do not like to change, and the less so as they do not see the evil staring them in the face, but presented to them as a mere conjecture.

As to reforming these institutions all at once when their defects have become manifest to everybody, that also is most difficult; for to do this, ordinary means will not suffice; they may even be injurious under such circumstances, and therefore it becomes necessary to resort to extraordinary measures, such as violence and arms, and above all things to make oneself absolute master of the state, so as to be able to dispose of it at will. And as the reformation of the political condition of a state presupposes a good man, while the making of himself prince of a republic by violence naturally presupposes a bad one, it will consequently be exceedingly rare that a good man should be found willing to employ wicked means to become a prince, even though his final object be good; or that a bad man, after having become prince, should be willing to labor for good ends, and that it should enter his mind to use for good purposes that authority which he has acquired by evil means. From these combined causes arises the difficulty or impossibility of maintaining liberty in a republic that has become corrupt, or to establish it there anew. And if it has to be introduced and maintained, then it will be necessary to reduce the state to a monarchical, rather than a republican form of government; for men whose turbulence could not be controlled by the simple force of law can be controlled in a measure only by an almost regal power. And to attempt to restore men to good conduct by any other means would be either a most cruel or an impossible undertaking. (*D*, I:18)

A republic that wishes to avoid the vice of ingratitude cannot employ the same means as a prince; that is to say, she cannot go and command her own expeditions, and is obliged therefore to confide them to some one of her citizens. But it is proper that I should suggest as the best means to adopt the same course that Rome did, in being less ungrateful than others and which resulted from her institutions. For as the whole city, nobles and plebeians, devoted themselves to the business of war, there arose at all times in Rome so many brave and victorious generals that the people had no cause for mistrusting any one of them, there being so many that they could watch each other. And thus they kept themselves so pure and careful not to give the least umbrage, that they afforded the people not the least ground for suspecting them of ambition; and if any of them arrived at the dictatorship, their greatest glory consisted in promptly laying this dignity down again; and thus having inspired no fear or mistrust, they gave no cause for ingratitude. A republic, then, that wishes not to have cause for ingratitude, should adopt the same system of government as Rome; and a citizen who desires to avoid the fangs of ingratitude should observe the same conduct as that of the Roman citizens. (*D*, I:30)

[H]ow well the institutions of that city [Rome] were calculated to make her great, and what an error other republics commit in deviating from her system. For although the Romans were great lovers of glory, yet they did not esteem it dishonorable to obey those whom they had at a previous time commanded, or to serve in that army of which they themselves had been chiefs. This custom is entirely contrary to the opinion, rules, and practice of our times; and in Venice they even yet hold to the error that a citizen who has once held a high post under the state would be dishonored by accepting a lower one; and the city consents to what she cannot change. However honorable this may be for a private citizen, yet for the public it is absolutely useless. (*D*, I:36)

The progress of the Roman republic demonstrates how difficult it is in the constitution of a republic to provide necessary laws for the maintenance of liberty. (*D*, I:49)

[E]ven in Rome, where the laws had been made by herself with the aid of her most sagacious citizens, every day fresh occasions arose that made it necessary to have new laws for the protection of liberty -- that in other cities whose beginnings were vicious such difficulties should present themselves as made a proper organization. (*D*, I:49)

[History] proves how much probity and religion these [Roman] people had, and how much good there was to be hoped for from them. And truly, where this probity does not exist, no good is to be expected, as in fact it is vain to look for anything good from those countries which we see nowadays so corrupt, as is the case above all others with Italy. (*D*, I:55)

For we know from many instances to what danger [the Romans] exposed themselves to preserve or recover their liberty, and what vengeance they practiced upon those who had deprived them of it. The lessons of history teach us also, on the other hand, the injuries people suffer from servitude. And while in our own times there is only one country in which we can say that free communities exist, in those ancient times all countries contained numerous cities that enjoyed similar liberty. (*D*, II:2)

And it was thus that the Romans never took any undecided middle course in important affairs . . . All princes and republics should imitate this example . . . (*D*, II:23)

If we observe carefully the course of human affairs, we shall often notice accidents and occurrences against which it seems to be the will of Heaven that we should not have provided. And if the events to which I refer occurred at Rome, where there was so much virtue, so much religion, and such order, it is no wonder that similar circumstances occur even much more frequently in a city or province deficient in the above advantages. (*D*, II:29)

It is noteworthy that . . . in the whole course of the existence of the Roman republic, the Romans never made any acquisitions by means of money; nor did they ever purchase a peace, but secured it always by the valor of their arms, which I do not believe can be said of any other republic.

Amongst the other indications by which the power of a republic may be recognized is the relation in which they live with their neighbors; if these are tributary to her by way of securing her friendship and protection, then it is a sure sign that the republic is powerful. But if these neighboring states, though they may be more feeble than herself, draw money from her, then it is a sure indication of great weakness on the part of the republic. (*D*, II:30)

Rome was a republic that produced citizens of various character and dispositions . . . It is this which assures to republics greater vitality and more enduring success than monarchies have; for the diversity of the genius of her citizens enables the republic better to accommodate herself to the changes of the times than can be done by a prince. For any man accustomed to a certain mode of proceeding will never change it . . . and consequently when time and circumstances change, so that his ways are no longer in harmony with them, he must of necessity succumb. (*D*, III:9)

[I]t is the common fault of republics in tranquil times to take small account of men of merit. And it is a twofold cause of indignation for such men to see themselves deprived of the rank to which they are entitled, and to be associated with, and often even subordinated to unworthy men, who are their inferiors in capacity. This defect in republics has often caused great evils; for those citizens who feel themselves so unjustly depreciated, and knowing it to be the result of the peace and tranquillity which the state enjoys, will stir up troubles and kindle fresh wars to the detriment of the republic.

In reflecting upon the means for remedying this evil, I believe I have found two. The first is to keep the citizens poor, so that their wealth and lack of virtue may neither corrupt themselves nor enable them to corrupt others; and the second, so to organize for war as to be ever prepared for it, as Rome did in her early days. For as this city always kept armies in the field, there was constant opportunity for the employment of men of ability; nor could rank be withheld from a man who deserved it, neither could it be bestowed upon another who did not merit it. And if, notwithstanding this, it was at times done, either by mistake or by way of trial, it caused at once such disorders and dangers that they quickly returned to the regular course. But other republics, which are not constituted like Rome, and who engage in war only when compelled by necessity, cannot avoid this inconvenience, but are rather constantly led into it. And this will always produce evil consequences whenever the meritorious citizen, who has thus been neglected, is disposed to be vindictive and has influence and partisans in the city. Rome avoided this evil practice for a time; but after she had conquered Carthage and Antioch . . . and no longer fearing other wars, she also seems to have confided the conduct of her armies indifferently to whoever aspired to it, looking less to the merits and ability of the man than to such other qualifications as assured him favor with the people. (*D*, III:16)

If we study carefully the conduct of the Roman republic, we discover two causes of her decadence; the one was the dissensions consequent upon the agrarian laws, and the other the prolongation of her military commands. If these matters had been better understood in the beginning, and proper remedies applied, the liberties of Rome would have endured longer, and she would probably have enjoyed great tranquillity. And although the prolongation of these powers does not seem to have engendered any actual disturbances, yet the facts show how injurious the authority which the citizens acquired thereby proved to civil liberty. But these inconveniences might have been avoided if those other citizens to whom the prolongation of the magistracies were conceded had been as wise and as virtuous as Lucius Quintius. His good qualities were indeed a notable example; for when an agreement had been concluded between the people and the Senate, and the military powers of the Tribunes had been extended by the people for one year in the belief that they would be able to restrain the ambition of the nobles, the Senate, from a spirit of rivalry and a desire not to appear less powerful than the people, wanted also to extend the term of the consulate of L. Quintius. But he absolutely opposed this determination, saying that they should strive rather to destroy the evil examples, than to add to their number by others and worse ones; and he demanded the creation of new Consuls. If the citizens of Rome generally had shared the virtue and prudence of L. Quintius, they would never have permitted the practice of the prolongation of the magistracies, which custom led to the prolongation of the military commands, which in time proved the ruin of the republic. . . Thus, if Rome had not prolonged the magistracies and the military commands, she might not so soon have attained the zenith of her power; but if she had been slower in her conquests, she would have also preserved her liberties the longer. (*D*, III:24)

We have argued elsewhere that it is of the greatest advantage in a republic to have laws that keep her citizens poor. Although there does not appear to have been any special law to this effect in Rome (the agrarian law having met with the greatest opposition), yet experience shows that even so late as four hundred years after its foundation there was still great poverty in Rome. We cannot ascribe this fact to any other cause than that poverty never was allowed to stand in the way of the achievement of any rank or honor, and that virtue and merit were sought for under whatever roof they dwelt; it was this system that made riches naturally less desirable. (*D*, III:25)

Now any republic that adopts the military organization and discipline of the Romans, and strives by constant training to give her soldiers experience and to develop their courage and mastery over fortune, will always and under all circumstances find them to display a courage and dignity similar to that of the Romans. But a republic unprovided with such military force, and which relies more upon the chances of fortune than upon the valor of her citizens, will experience all the vicissitudes of fortune, and will have the same fate as the Venetians.(*D*, III:31)

We have already said elsewhere, that in a great republic there are constantly evils occurring requiring remedies which must be efficacious in proportion to the importance of the occasion. And if ever any city experienced strange and unforeseen ills it was Rome. (*D*, III:49)

For when any crime is committed by a multitude, where the individual authors cannot be ascertained, it is impossible to punish them all, there being so many. To chastise a part, leaving the others unpunished, would be unjust to the first, while the others would feel encouraged to commit fresh crimes. But where all have merited death, and only every tenth man is punished by lot, these will have occasion to complain only of fate; while those who escape will be careful not to commit other crimes, for fear that the next time the lot might fall to them. . . .

Although the consequences of such evils in a republic are bad, yet they are not mortal, for there is always time to correct them. But it is not the same with such evils as affect the state itself; for unless they are checked and corrected by some wise hand, they will cause the ruin of the state. The liberality with which the Romans used to grant the privileges of citizenship to strangers had attracted a great many new families to Rome. These began to exercise so great an influence in the elections that it sensibly changed the government, and caused it to deviate from the institutions and principles of the men who had been accustomed to direct it. When Quintius Fabius, who as Censor at that time, observed this, he had all the new families that had caused this disorder enrolled into four tribes; so that, being confined to such narrow limits, they should not corrupt Rome. Fabius had well comprehended the evil, and promptly and without difficulty applied a suitable remedy; which was so well received by the republic, that it earned him the surname Maximus. (*D*, III:49)

The serious and natural enmities between the people and the nobles, caused by the latter's wish to rule and the former's not be enthralled, bring about all the evils that spring up in cities; by this opposition of parties all the other things that disturb republics are nourished. This kept Rome disunited. This (if small things with great may be compared) has kept Florence divided, though in the two cities diverse effects were produced, because the enmities that at the outset existed in Rome between the people and the nobles were ended by debating, those in Florence by fighting; those in Rome were terminated by law, those in Florence by the exile and death of many citizens; those in Rome always increased military power, those in Florence wholly destroyed it; those in Rome brought that city from an equality of citizens to a very great inequality; those in Florence brought her from inequality to a striking equality.

It must be that this difference of effects was caused by the different purposes of these two peoples, for the people of Rome wished to enjoy supreme honors along with the nobles; the people of Florence fought to be alone in the government, without any participation in it by the nobles. Because the Roman people's desire was more reasonable, their injuries to the nobles were more endurable, so that the nobility yielded easily and without coming to arms; hence, after some debates, they agreed in making a law with which the people would be satisfied and by which the nobles would remain in their public offices. On the other hand, the Florentine people's desire was harmful and unjust, so that the nobility with greater forces prepared to defend themselves, and therefore the result was blood and the exile of citizens, and the laws then made were planned not for the common profit but altogether in favor of the conqueror. From this it also resulted that through the people's victories, the city of Rome became more excel-lent, because along with nobles, men from the people could be appointed to administer the magistracies, the armies, and the high offices; thus the latter acquired the same ability the former had, and that city, as she increased in excellence, increased in power. But in Florence, since the people won, the nobles continued to be deprived of high offices, and if they wished to get them again, they were forced in their conduct, their spirit, and their way of living not merely to be like the men of the people, but to seem so. From this came the changes in ensigns, the alterations in the titles of families that the nobles carried out in order to seem like the people. Hence the ability in arms and the boldness of spirit possessed by the nobility were destroyed, and these qualities could not be rekindled in the people, where they did not exist, so that Florence grew always weaker and more despicable. Whereas Rome, when that excellence of her citizens was turned into pride, was brought to such a pass that she could not keep going without a prince, Florence has come to such a condition that easily a wise lawgiver, could reorganize her with almost any form of govern-ment. (*HF*, III:1)

And as long as the Roman republic continued incorrupt, no citizen, however powerful, ever presumed to avail himself of that profession in peacetime so as to trample upon the laws, to plunder provinces, or to turn tyrant and enslave his country; nor did any private soldier dare to violate his oath, to enter into faction and cabals, to throw off his allegiance to the Senate, or to support any tyrannical attempt upon the liberties of the commonwealth in order to enable himself to live by the profession of arms at all times. The commanders, on the contrary, contenting themselves with the honor of a triumph, returned with eagerness to their former manner of living; and the common soldiers laid down their arms with much more pleasure than they had taken them up. Each resumed the calling by which he had gotten his bread before, and none had any hopes of advancing himself by plunder and rapine. (*AW*, I)

And if we consider the practice and institutions observed by the old Romans (whose example I am always fond of recommending), we shall find many things worthy of imitation; these may easily be introduced into any other state, if it has not become totally corrupt. . . : To honor and reward *virtù*, not to scorn poverty, to value good order and discipline in their armies, to oblige citizens to love one another, to decline faction, and to prefer the good of the public to any private interest; and other such principles which would be compatible enough with these times. These principles might easily be introduced if due means were taken for that purpose because they appear so reasonable in themselves, and because their expediency is so obvious to common sense that nobody could gainsay or oppose them. (*AW*, I)

[A]s long as Rome continued to be well-governed (which was until the time of the Gracchi) there was never any soldier who made war his only occupation; and so it happened that few of them were dissolute or licentious -- and those few were severely punished.

Every well-governed commonwealth, therefore, should take care that this art of war should be practiced in time of peace only as an exercise, and in time of war, only out of necessity and for the acquisition of glory, and that it should be practiced, as in Rome, by the state alone. For if any citizen has another end or design in following this profession, he is not a good man; if any commonwealth acts otherwise, it is not well-governed. (*AW*, I)

But where there are severe punishments, there should also be proportionate rewards to excite men to behave themselves well from motives of both hope and fear; therefore, [the Romans] always rewarded those who had distinguished themselves by any meritorious action, especially those who had saved the life of a fellow citizen in battle, had been the first in scaling the walls of an enemy's town or storming their camp, or had wounded, killed, or unhorsed an enemy. In this manner, each man's desert was properly taken notice of, recompensed by the consuls, and honored publicly; those who obtained any reward for services of this kind, besides the reputation and glory which they acquired among their fellow soldiers, were, when they returned from the wars, received by their friends and relations with all kinds of rejoicings and congratulations. It is no wonder, then, that a people who were so exact in rewarding merit and punishing offenders should extend their empire to such a degree as they did; they are certainly highly worthy of imitation in these respects. (*AW*, VI)

VII. Corruption and Renewal

But -- whether it proceeds from mankind's ignorance, inattention, or indolence, I know not -- it is certain that bad customs are seldom changed, no matter who is at the helm or whatever example may be brought either to discredit such customs or to recommend their contraries. (*AW*, I)

Unhappy . . . is that republic which, not having at the beginning fallen into the hands of a sagacious and skillful legislator, is herself obliged to reform her laws. More unhappy still is that republic which from the first has diverged from a good constitution. And that republic is furthest from happiness whose vicious institutions impede her progress, and make her leave the right path that leads to a good end; for those who are in that condition can hardly ever be brought into the right road. Those republics, on the other hand, that started without having even a perfect constitution, but made a fair beginning and are capable of improvement; such republics, I say, may perfect themselves by the aid of events. It is very true, however, that such reforms are never effected without danger, for the majority of men never willingly adopt any new law tending to change the constitution of the state, unless the necessity of the change is clearly demonstrated; and as such a necessity cannot make itself felt without being accompanied with danger, the republic may easily be destroyed before having perfected its constitution. (*D*, I:2)

And truly, if a price be anxious for glory and the good opinion of the world, he should rather wish to possess a corrupt city, not to ruin it like Caesar, but to reorganize it like Romulus. For certainly the heavens cannot afford a man a greater opportunity of glory, nor could men desire a better one. And if for the proper organization of a city it should be necessary to abolish the principality, he who had failed to give her good laws for the sake of preserving his rank may be entitled to some excuse; but there would be none for him who had been able to organize the city properly and yet preserve the sovereignty. And in fine, let him to whom Heaven has vouchsafed such an opportunity, reflect that there are two ways open to him; one that will enable him to live securely and insure him glory after death, and the other that will make his life one of constant anxiety, and after death consign him to eternal infamy. (*D*, I:10)

He who desires or attempts to reform the government of a state, and wishes to have it accepted and capable of maintaining itself to the satisfaction of everybody, must at least retain the semblance of the old forms; so that it may seem to the people that there has been no change in the institutions, even though in fact they are entirely different from the old ones. For the great majority of mankind are satisfied with appearances as though they were realities, and are often even more influenced by the things that seem than by those that are. . . . And this rule should be observed by all who wish to abolish an existing system of government in any state, and introduce a new and more liberal one. For as all novelties excite the minds of men, it is important to retain in such innovations as much as possible the previously existing forms. And if the number, authority, and duration of the term of service of the magistrates be changed, the titles at least ought to be preserved. This, as I have said, should be observed by whoever desires to convert an absolute government either into a republic or a monarchy; but on the contrary, he who wishes to establish an absolute power, such as ancient writers called a tyranny, must change everything . . . (*D*, I:25)

[I]f a city, which from its origin has enjoyed liberty but has of itself become corrupt, has great difficulties in devising good laws for the maintenance of liberty, it is not to be wondered at if a city that had its origin in servitude finds it not only difficult, but actually impossible ever to organize a government that will secure its liberty and tranquillity. (*D*, I:49)

There is nothing more true than that all the things of this world have a limit to their existence; but those only run the entire course ordained for them by Heaven that do not allow their body to become disorganized, but keep it unchanged in the manner ordained, or if they change it, so do it that it shall be for their advantage and not to their injury. And as I speak here of mixed bodies, such as republics or religious sects, I say that those changes are beneficial that bring them back to their original principles. And those are the best constituted bodies and have the longest existence, which possess the intrinsic means of frequently renewing themselves, or such as obtain this renovation in consequence of some extrinsic accidents. And it is a truth clearer than light that, without such renovation, these bodies cannot continue to exist; and the means of renewing them is to bring them back to their original principles. For as all religious republics and monarchies must have within themselves some goodness by means of which they obtain their first growth and reputation, and as in the process of time this goodness becomes corrupted, it will of necessity destroy the body unless something intervenes to bring it back to its normal condition.

Thus, the doctors of medicine say in speaking of the human body, that "every day some ill humors gather which must be cured."

This return of a republic to its original principles is either the result of extrinsic accident or of intrinsic prudence. As an instance of the first, we have seen how necessary it was that Rome should be taken by the Gauls as a means of her renovation or new birth; so that, being thus born again, she might take new life and vigor, and might resume the proper observance of justice and religion which were becoming corrupt. . . . [Rome] needed . . . this blow from without to revive the observance of all the institutions of the state, and to show to the Roman people, not only the necessity of maintaining religion and justice, but also of honoring their good citizens and making more account of their virtue than of the ease and indulgence of which their energy and valor seemed to deprive them. . . .

It is necessary then . . . for men who live associated together under some kind of regulations, often to be brought back to themselves, so to speak, either by external or internal occurrences. As to the latter, they are either the result of a law that obliges the citizens of the association often to render an account of their conduct; or some man of superior character arises amongst them, whose noble example and virtuous actions will produce the same effect as such a law. This good, then, in a republic is due either to the excellence of some one man, or to some law; and as to the latter, the institution that brought the Roman Republic back to its original principles was the creation of the Tribunes of the people, and all the other laws that tended to repress the insolence and ambition of men. But to give life and vigor to those laws requires a virtuous citizen, who will courageously aid in their execution against the power of those who transgress them. . . .

As these were extreme and most striking cases, they caused on each occasion a return of the citizens to the original principles of the republic; and when they began to be more rare, it also began to afford men more latitude in becoming corrupt, and the execution of the laws involved more danger and disturbances. It would be desirable, therefore, that not more than ten years should elapse between such executions, for in the long course of time men begin to change their customs, and to transgress the laws; and unless some case occurs that recalls the punishment to their memory and revives the fear in their hearts, the delinquents will soon become so numerous that they cannot be punished without danger.

In relation to this subject it was said by the magistrates who governed Florence from the year 1434 until 1494 [when the Medici ruled the city] that it was necessary every five years to resume the government, and that otherwise it would be difficult to maintain it. By "resuming the government" they meant to strike the people with the same fear and terror as they did when they first assumed the government, and when they had inflicted the extremist punishment upon those who, according to their principles, had conducted themselves badly. But as the recollection of these punishments fades from men's minds, they become emboldened to make new attempts against the government, and to speak ill of it, and therefore it is necessary to provide against this, by bringing the government back to its first principles. Such a return to first principles in a republic is sometimes caused by the simple virtues of one man, without depending upon any law that incites him to the infliction of extreme punishments; and yet his good example has such an influence that the good men strive to imitate him, and the wicked are ashamed to lead a life so contrary to his example. . . . And certainly if at least some such signal punishments as described above, or noble examples, had occurred in Rome every ten years, that city never would have become corrupt; but as both became more rare, corruption increased more and more. . . .

We conclude, then, that nothing is more necessary for an association of men, either as a religious sect, republic, or monarchy, than to restore to it from time to time the power and reputation which it had in the beginning, and to strive to have either good laws or good men to bring about such a result, without the necessity of the intervention of any extrinsic force. For although such may at time be the best remedy . . . yet it is so dangerous that it is in no way desirable. (*D*, III:1)

That we cannot thus change at will is due to two causes: the one is the impossibility of resisting the natural bent of our characters, and the other is the difficulty of persuading ourselves, after having been accustomed to success by a certain mode of proceeding, that any other can succeed as well. It is this that causes the varying success of a man; for the times change, but he does not change his mode of proceeding. The ruin of states is caused in a like manner . . . because they do not modify their institutions to suit the changes of the times. And such changes are more difficult and tardy in republics; for necessarily circumstances will occur that will unsettle the whole state, and when the change of proceeding of one man will not suffice for the occasion. (*D*, III:9)

[A]s all human institutions . . . contain some inherent evil that gives rise to unforeseen accidents, it becomes necessary to provide against these by new measures. (*D*, III:11)

A republic would be perpetual that has the good fortune often to find men who by their example restore the laws to their original purity and force . . . and not only prevent her from falling into decadence, but rather carry her in the opposite direction. (*D*, III:13)

To usurp supreme and absolute authority . . . in a free state, and subject it to tyranny, the people must have already become corrupt by gradual steps from generation to generation. And all states necessarily come to this, unless . . . they are frequently reinvigorated by good examples, and brought back to good laws to their first principles. . . . And therefore all such as desire to make a change in the government of a republic, whether in favor of liberty or in favor of tyranny, must well examine the condition of things, and from that judge of the difficulties of their undertaking. For it is as difficult to make a people free that is resolved to live in servitude, as it is to subject a people to servitude that is determined to be free . . . [I]n any such attempts men should well consider the state of the times and govern themselves accordingly . . . (*D*, III:8)

In their normal variations, countries generally go from order to disorder and then from disorder move back to order because -- since nature does not allow worldly things to remain fixed -- when they come to their utmost perfection and have no further possibility for rising, they must go down. Likewise, when they have gone down and through their defects have reached the lowest depths, they necessarily rise, since they cannot go lower. So always from good they go down to bad, and from bad rise up to good. Because ability brings forth quiet; quiet, laziness; laziness, disorder; disorder, ruin; and likewise from ruin comes order; from order, ability; from the last, glory and good fortune. Therefore the discerning have noted that letters come after arms, and that in countries and cities generals are born earlier than philosophers. Because after good and well-disciplined armies have brought forth victory, and their victories quiet, the virtue of military courage cannot be corrupted with a more honorable laziness than that of letters; nor with a greater and more dangerous deception can this laziness enter into well-regulated cities. When the philosophers Diogenes and Carneades came to Rome, sent by the Athenians as ambassadors to the Senate, Cato thoroughly realized this; hence, seeing that the Roman youth began to follow them with admiration, and knowing the evil that such honorable laziness might bring upon his country, he made a law that no philosopher should be received in Rome. By such means, then, countries come to ruin; and when they have suffered it, and their people through afflictions have grown wise, they return to good order, as I have said, unless indeed an unusual force keeps them stifled. (*HF*, V:1)

Glossary

Agrarian Law Reform measure proposed by Roman tribune Tiberius Gracchus in 133 B.C. The law sought to limit the holding of public land to 300 acres per person, pay present landholders for any improvements they had made, and rent the remaining land to the poorer classes of citizens. Opposition was immediate and fierce among the rich landlords, who looked upon the measure as an unwarranted confiscation and redistribution of their property. The efforts of Tiberius and his brother Gaius at agrarian reform did not produce any lasting effect, but did unleash the forces of class warfare, which set the stage for the great civil conflicts that followed.

Alexander the Great (356-323 B.C.) King of Macedon, son of Philip II, and military conqueror who helped spread Greek culture to Asia Minor, Egypt, and India.

Assembly Popular body through which Roman citizens elected magistrates and approved or rejected such proposals as the consuls put before it. The assembly's powers were limited to voting, and it did not have the right to initiate legislation or to discuss or amend measures presented to it. The assemblies legislative power was, moreover, limited by the Senate's power of veto.

Aristotle (384-322 B.C.) Greek philosopher who studied under Plato at the Academy, tutor to Alexander the Great, and founder of his own school, the Lyceum. His treatise on *Politics* is one of the most influential works in the field.

Brutus, Lucius Junius (c. 510 B.C.) Roman patriot who according to tradition led the Roman people in driving the last Tarquin king from Rome. When his sons were implicated in a conspiracy to restore the monarchy, Brutus (who had become Rome's first consul in 509 B.C.) ordered their deaths.

Caesar, Julius Gaius (100-44 B.C.) Roman patrician, general, statesman, and author. His dictatorship marked the end of the Roman republic.

Carneades (c. 213-128 B.C.) Skeptical Greek philosopher and head of Academy founded by Plato. He accompanied the Stoic philosopher Diogenes on an embassy to Rome in 156 B.C.

Cato, Marcus Porcius (234-149 B.C.) Roman statesmen and "Censor," who considered philosophy inconsistent with military virtue. When the lectures of some visiting Greek philosophers caused a sensation among the Roman youth, he advised the Senate to dismiss them as soon as possible.

Censor One of two Roman magistrates elected by the assembly for an eighteen month term. Originally the censors were appointed to take the census and assess land values. Later they were authorized to sit in judgment of the qualifications of senators, which involved the supervision of their public and private conduct.

Cicero, Marcus Tullius (106-43 B.C.) Roman statesman, orator, and philosopher. He was put to death by order of Marc Antony following the murder of Julius Caesar.

Consul One of two chief Roman magistrates who alternated in the exercise of the office. Elected by the assembly for a one-year term, the consul presided over the Senate and popular assemblies, and had the sole right of bringing important measures before the latter. Each consul could veto the proposals of the other. The nomination of the dictator was also entrusted to the consul. Only patricians were eligible to hold the consulship.

Dante Alighieri (1265-1321) Italian poet and author of *The Divine Comedy*. He also wrote a political treatise, *On Monarchy*, during his exile from his native Florence.

Decemvirs Roman council of ten magistrates which in 451 B.C. drew up the Twelve Tables, the first Roman code of law. When the patrician led council refused to resign after completing its work, the army and a multitude of citizens withdrew from the city, thus jeopardizing the security of the state. This measure forced the Decemvirs out of power, and the old government was restored.

Dictator Roman magistrate with supreme authority appointed by the consuls in times of emergency. The dictator, who was typically engaged in military tasks, was expected to lay down his office when the crisis had passed. The maximum term was six months, and the dictator was never held responsible for his conduct.

Diogenes of Seleucia (c. 155) Stoic philosopher who accompanied Carneades to Rome as part of an Athenian embassy.

Fabius, Quintus (c. 260-203 B.C.) Roman statesman and general appointed dictator during the second Punic War who adopted a "Fabian" strategy of cautious delay and avoidance of direct encounter. He opposed Scipio's more aggressive policy, including his invasion of northern Africa.

Gracchi Gaius (c. 153-121 B.C.) and Tiberius Gracchus (c. 163-133 B.C.) Roman statesmen and social reformers. As tribune Tiberius proposed the so-called "agrarian law," which was passed illegally and in opposition to the senate. He was killed in the Forum, along with three hundred of his followers, during a riot incited by the senatorial class. Gaius continued his brother's reform efforts, securing the passage of the "corn law" which allowed the poor to obtain public stores of grain at low cost. He lost his life in a tumult in which three thousand citizens were slain.

Herod (c. 73-4 B.C.) King of Judea by nomination of Rome. He was a capable administrator, but unpopular with the Jews for his policy of Hellenization. Herod eventually alienated Caesar Augustus by the brutal murders of his family at the end of his reign.

Lycurgus (c. 850 B.C.) Legendary Spartan lawgiver who according to tradition established the constitution and military regime of Sparta.

Marius, Gaius (157-86 B.C.) Roman general and statesman who defeated Jugurtha in Africa and Celtic tribes in northern Italy. Highly popular with the plebeians, he was repeatedly elected consul, and led the extreme democrats against the patricians. This conflict led to the first of the civil wars between military leaders, which ended in the collapse of the Roman republic.

Numa Pompilius (c. 715-672) Second of seven kings of Roman tradition and semi-mythical founder of the Roman religious system and calender.

Philip II (382-336 B.C.) King of Macedon and father of Alexander the Great. He made Macedon a major power and created a highly-trained professional army. Philip extended his sphere of influence by skillfully exploiting the dissensions between the Greek city-states.

Pisistratus (c.600-524) A tyrant of Athens under whose benevolent despotism the city developed culturally and economically. He retained the constitution of Solon and prepared the way for the democratic reforms of his successors.

Plato (428-348) Greek philosopher who as a young man was a follower of Socrates. Later he founded the Academy in Athens, where he taught for forty years. His principal works on politics are *The Republic* and *The Laws*.

Preaetoriate Annually elected Roman magistracy created after the restoration of the consulship in 366 B.C. The praetor was regarded as a junior colleague of the consuls. He could take command of an army, convene the Senate or assembly, and exercise the other consular functions.

Romulus (c.776) Legendary founder of Rome who according to tradition killed his brother Remus, and reigned for the next forty years as the city's first king.

Scipio, Africanus Major (236-184 B.C.) Roman general and statesman, and hero of the second Punic War. He defeated Hannibal at the battle of Zama, and latter served twice as consul.

Senate Roman council composed of 300 members drawn primarily from the patrician class. Its principal duty was to act as an advisory body to the consuls, who were typically reluctant to act contrary to the Senate's advice. The Senate acquired the right to sanction or veto resolutions passed by the assembly, which could not become laws without the Senate's approval. The composition of the Senate and the life tenure its members made it a strongly conservative body devoted to maintaining the interests of the patrician aristocracy.

Solon (c. 640-560) Athenian statesman and lawgiver whose famous reforms laid the foundation of democracy in Athens.

Tarquins Etruscan kings who ruled Rome prior to the Republic. The last Tarquin king was driven out of the city by the Roman people under the leadership of L. Junius Brutus in 509 B.C.

Titus Livius (59 B.C.-17 A.D.) Roman historian and author of a famous history of Rome. Of its 142 books only thirty-five and a few fragments survive. Machiavelli's *Discourses* is ostensibly a commentary on the first ten books of Livy's history.

Tribune One of ten Roman magistrates elected by the assembly to protect the interests and rights of the plebeians against violations by the patricians. The tribune was authorized to inflict punishment, including death, on a magistrate who persisted in wrongdoing, and could pass immediate sentence on anyone who violated the sanctity of his person. Only plebeians qualified for the tribunate.

Selected Bibliography
of Works on Machiavelli

Allen, J. W., "Machiavelli," in *A History of Political Thought in the Sixteenth Century* (New York, 1928), 447-494.

Anglo, Sydney, *Machiavelli: A Dissection* (London, 1969).

Barincou, Edmond, *Machiavelli*, trans. Helen R. Lane (New York, 1961).

Baron, Hans, "Machiavelli: The Republican Citizen and the Author the 'The Prince'," *English Historical Review*, 76 (1961), 217-253.

Berlin, Isiah, "The Originality of Machiavelli," in *Against the Current: Essays in the History of Ideas* (London, 1979), 25-79.

Bock, Gisela, et al., ed., *Machiavelli and Republicanism* (Cambridge, Eng., 1990).

Bonadeo, Alfredo, *Corruption, Conflict, and Power in the Works and Times of Niccolò Machiavelli* (Berkeley, 1973).

_____, "The Role of the 'Grandi' in the Political World of Machiavelli," *Studies in the Renaissance*, 16 (1969), 21-25.

_____, "Machiavelli on Civic Equality and Republican Government," *Romance Notes*, 11 (1969), 160-166.

_____, "The Role of the People in the Works and Times of Machiavelli," *Bibliothèque d'humanisme et renaissance*, 32 (1970), 351-377.

Bondanella, Peter E., *Machiavelli and the Art of Renaissance History* (Detroit, 1973).

Burd, L. A., "Florence (II): Machiavelli," in *The Cambridge Modern History*, vol. 1, ed., A. W. Ward, et al., (Cambridge, Eng., 1934), 190-218.

Burnham, James, "Machiavelli: The Science of Power," in *The Machiavellians, Defenders of Freedom* (New York, 1973), 20-58.

Butterfield, Herbert, *The Statecraft of Machiavelli* (Oxford, 1947).

Butters, Humphrey, "Good Government and the Limitations of Power in the Writings of Niccolò Machiavelli," *History of Political Thought*, 7 (1986), 411-417.

Campbell, William R., "Machiavelli's Anthropology of Obligation: The Politics of Morality," *Polity*, 4 (1972), 449-478.

Cassirer, Ernst, *The Myth of the State* (New Haven, 1946), 116-162.

Chabod, Federico, *Machiavelli and the Renaissance*, trans. David Moore (London, 1958).

Clough, Cecil, "Niccolò Machiavelli's Political Assumptions and Objectives," *Bulletin of the John Rylands Library*, 53 (1970), 30-74.

Cochrane, Eric W., "Machiavelli: 1940-1960," *Journal of Modern History*, 33 (1961), 112-136.

Colish, Marcia L., "The Idea of Liberty in Machiavelli," *Journal of the History of Ideas*, 32 (1971), 323-350.

de Grazia, Sebastian, *Machiavelli in Hell* (Princeton, 1989).

Eldar, Dan, "Glory and the Boundaries of Public Morality in Machiavelli's Thought," *History of Political Thought*, 7 (1986), 419-438.

Fleisher, Martin, "The Ways of Machiavelli and the Ways of Politics," *History of Political Thought*, 16 (1995), 330-335.

_____, ed., *Machiavelli and the Nature of Political Thought* (New York, 1972).

Friedrich, Carl J., "Machiavelli: The State as a Work of Art and its Rationality," in *Constitutional Reason of State: The Survival of the Constitutional Order* (Providence, R. I., 1957), 15-33.

Garver, Eugene, "After *Virtú*: Rhetoric, Prudence, and Moral Pluralism in Machiavelli," *History of Political Thought*, 17 (1996), 195-222.

_____, *Machiavelli and the History of Prudence* (Madison, Wis., 1987).

Geerken, John H., "Machiavelli Studies Since 1969," *Journal of the History of Ideas*, 37 (1976), 351-368.

Gilbert, Felix, "The Composition and Structure of Machiavelli's *Discoursi*," *Journal of the History of Ideas*, 14 (1953), 136-156.

_____, "Machiavellism," in *History: Choice and Commitment* (Cambridge, Mass., 1977), 155-176.

_____, *Machiavelli and Guicciardini: Politics and History in Sixteenth-Century Florence* (Princeton, 1965).

Gilmore, Myron P., ed., *Studies on Machiavelli* (Florence, 1972).

Hannaford, I., "Machiavelli's Concept of *Virtú* in *The Prince* and *The Discourses* Reconsidered," *Political Studies*, 20 (1972), 185-189.

Hulliung, Mark, *Citizen Machiavelli* (Princeton, 1983).

Ingersoll, David E., "Machiavelli and Madison: Perspectives on Political Stability," *Political Science Quarterly*, 85 (1970), 259-280.

_____, "The Constant Prince: Private Interests and Public Goals in Machiavelli," *Western Political Quarterly*, 21 (1968), 588-596.

Kraft, Joseph, "Truth and Poetry in Machiavelli," *Journal of Modern History*, 23 (1951), 109-121.

Macaulay, Thomas B., "Machiavelli," in *Critical, Historical, and Miscellaneous Essays and Poems*, vol. 1. (Chicago, 1889), 193-230

McCormick, John P., "Addressing the Political Exception: Machiavelli's 'Accidents' and the Mixed Regime," *American Political Science Review*, 87 (1993), 888-900.

McCoy, Charles N. R., "The Place of Machiavelli in the History of Political Thought," *American Political Science Review*, 37 (1943), 626-641.

Mansfield, Harvey C., Jr., *Machiavelli's Virtue* (Chicago, 1996).

_____, *Machiavelli's New Modes and Orders: A Study of the Discourses on Livy* (Ithaca, N. Y., 1979).

Meinecke, Friedrich, "Machiavelli," in *Machiavellism: The Doctrine of Raison d'Etat and its Place in Modern History*, trans. Douglas Scott (New Haven, 1957), 25-48.

Muir, D. Erskine, *Machiavelli and His Times* (London, 1936).

Najemy, John M., "Baron's Machiavelli and Renaissance Republicanism," *American Historical Review*, 101 (1996), 119-129.

Newell, W. R., "How Original is Machiavelli?," *Political Theory*, 15 (1987), 612-634.

Olschki, Leonard, *Machiavelli the Scientist* (Berkeley, 1945).

Orwin, Clifford, "Machiavelli's Unchristian Charity," *American Political Science Review*, 72 (1978), 1217-1228.

Parel, Anthony J., ed., *The Political Calculus: Essays on Machiavelli's Philosophy* (Toronto, 1972).

_____, "Machiavelli's Notions of Justice: Text and Analysis," *Political Theory*, 18 (1990), 528-544.

_____, "The Question of Machiavelli's Modernity," *Review of Politics*, 53 (1991), 320-339.

Peterman, Larry, "Gravity and Piety: Machiavelli's Modern Turn," *Review of Politics*, 52 (1990), 189-214.

Pitkin, Hanna, *Fortune is a Woman: Gender and Politics in the Thought of Niccolò Machiavelli* (Berkeley, 1984).

Plamenatz, John, "Machiavelli," in *Man and Society, Political and Social Theory: Machiavelli through Rousseau* (New York, 1963), 2-44.

Preus, J. Samuel, "Machiavelli's Functional Analysis of Religion: Context and Object," *Journal of the History of Ideas*, 40 (1979), 171-190.

Prezzolini, Giuseppe, *Machiavelli*, trans. Gioconda Savini (New York, 1967).

Price, Russell, "The Senses of *Virtù* in Machiavelli," *European Studies Review*, 3 (1973), 315-345.

_____, "The Theme of *Gloria* in Machiavelli," *Renaissance Quarterly*, 30 (1977), 588-631.

_____, "*Ambizione* in Machiavelli's Thought," *History of Political Thought*, 3 (1982), 383-445.

_____, "Self-Love, 'Egoism' and *Ambizione* in Machiavelli's Thought," *History of Political Thought*, 9 (1988), 237-261.

Ridolofi, Roberto, *The Life of Niccolò Machiavelli*, trans. Cecil Grayson (New York, 1963).

Ruffo-Fiore, Silvia, *Niccolò Machiavelli* (Boston, 1982).

Savigear, Peter, "Niccolò Machiavelli: *The Prince* and the *Discourses*," in *A Guide to the Political Classics: Plato to Rousseau*, ed., Murray Forsyth and Maurice Keens-Soper (Oxford, 1988), 96-119

Sereno, Renzo, "A Falsification by Machiavelli," *Renaissance News*, 12 (1959), 159-167.

Shumer, S. M., "Machiavelli: Republican Politics and Its Corruption," *Political Theory*, 7 (1979), 5-34.

Skinner, Quentin, *Machiavelli* (New York, 1981).

Smith, Bruce J., "Machiavelli: Remembrance and the Republic," in *Politics and Remembrance: Republican Theories in Machiavelli, Burke, and Tocqueville* (Princeton, 1985), 26-101.

Stephens, J. N. and Butters, H. C., "New Light on Machiavelli," *English Historical Review*, 97 (1982), 54-69.

Strauss, Leo, *Thoughts on Machiavelli* (Chicago, 1958).

Sullivan, Vickie B., "Machiavelli's Momentary 'Machiavellian Moment': A Reconsideration of Pocock's Treatment of the *Discourses*," *Political Theory*, 20 (1992), 309-318.

_____, "Neither Christian Nor Pagan: Machiavelli's Treatment of Religion in the *Discourses*," *Polity*, 26 (1993), 259-280.

_____, *Machiavelli's Three Romes: Religion, Human Liberty, and Politics Reformed* (DeKalb, Ill., 1996).

Tarlton, Charles D., *Fortune's Circle: A Biographical Interpretation of Niccolò Machiavelli* (Chicago, 1970).

Tsurutani, Taketsugu, "Machiavelli and the Problem of Political Development," *Review of Politics*, 30 (1968), 316-330.

Walker, Leslie J., *The Discourses of Niccolò Machiavelli*, 2 vols. (London, 1950).

Wasley, Daniel, "The Primitivist Element in Machiavelli's Thought," *Journal of the History of Ideas*, 31 (1970), 91-98.

Whitfield, J. H., *Discourses on Machiavelli* (Cambridge, Eng., 1969).

_____, *Machiavelli* (Oxford, 1947).

Wolin, Sheldon S., "Machiavelli and the Economy of Violence," in *Politics and Vision: Continuity and Innovation in Western Political Theory* (Boston, 1960), 195-238.

Wood, Neal, "Machiavelli's Concept of *Virtù* Reconsidered," *Political Studies*, 15 (1967), 159-172.

Note on the Author

Quentin P. Taylor is an independent scholar who received a Ph.D. in political science at the University of Missouri (1992). In addition to Machiavelli, he has written on Plato, Augustine, Nietzsche, and *The Federalist Papers*. Currently he is writing a book on the foundations of the American republic. Dr. Taylor lives with his wife Lori in Midland, Texas.